Mexican History

A Captivating Guide to the History of Mexico and the Mexican Revolution

Free Bonus from Captivating History
(Available for a Limited time)

Hi History Lovers!

Now you have a chance to join our exclusive history list so you can get your first history ebook for free as well as discounts and a potential to get more history books for free! Simply visit the link below to join.

Captivatinghistory.com/ebook

Also, make sure to follow us on Facebook, Twitter and Youtube by searching for Captivating History.

Contents

Part 1: HISTORY OF MEXICO

A Captivating Guide to Mexican History, Starting from the Rise of Tenochtitlan through Maximilian's Empire to the Mexican Revolution and the Zapatista Indigenous Uprising

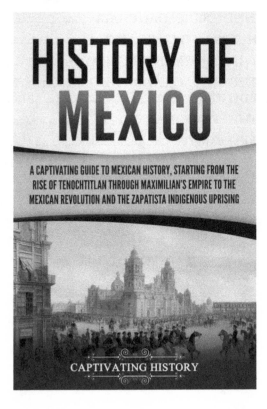

Introduction

Mexico is one of the most distinguishable shapes from space. The country's flag, of green, white, and red fields, contains the image of an eagle with spread wings standing on a cactus. Like few flags in the world, which mostly have celestial objects or colors representing ideals, Mexico's flag has terrestrial imagery, two animals—an eagle and a snake—and a historic moment: the moment when a group of emigrants called the Mexica arrived in the Valley of Mexico. The basin was full of interconnected lakes and snow-capped volcanoes, and it was where the newcomers saw a great bird in the center of the largest body of water. The city of Tenochtitlan, modern-day Mexico City, was founded on that site.

Other flags of the world have animals, mostly birds, as is the case of Mexico's, which traditionally represent freedom, might, or contact with the heavens. But certainly, no other flag has a snake, which is typically a representation of evil. For Mexicans, who are educated since childhood in its meaning, the symbol of the Mexican flag sums up the eternal and historic struggle between two forces, a destructive one, which seems to be intimately woven into the country's character, and a liberating and magnanimous one.

Like most flags of the world, Mexico's insignia speaks of its mythical origins. The image of the eagle on the cactus and the prickly pears, besides being an important moment in the history of the land and a motif that whispers deeply to the psyche of every Mexican, is also a reminder that before an independent country called Mexico existed, there were great cities in its valleys, jungles, and on its lakes— yes, *on* its lakes—which formed empires. Original civilizations arose in very few places on the planet without learning from other cultures, and as such, these people living in isolation from other societies created numerical systems, a writing system, and their own lifestyle in an autonomous and different way. Mexico was one of those places. Before the modern country was born in 1821, the territory that today comprises 32 states and few small islands was inhabited by ancient dynasties and kingdoms of warriors, astronomers, priests, temples for human sacrifice, and, surprisingly, some of the largest cities in the world. It is estimated that the sacred city of Chichen Itza, in the Yucatan Peninsula, was larger than Paris at its height of splendor. This fascinating journey through Mexico's history, from its amazing pre-Hispanic past to the end of the 20th century, will reveal more surprises than the reader can imagine. In the words of the self-proclaimed Mexican singer Chavela Vargas, "Mexico has magic. I looked for that magic, and I found it there."

Chapter 1 – The Era of Empires

Long before the emergence of empires in ancient Mexico, the first humans arrived from the north, descending along the western coast of North America or sailing along the seashore southward approximately thirteen thousand years ago. The first settlers surely arrived in intermittent small bands and settled mostly in the region now known as Mesoamerica, in southern Mexico and Central America. Approximately seven thousand years ago, the first seeds were harvested.

The first great civilization in the American continent arose in Mexico at the same time as the Babylonians in Asia, the so-called Olmecs, in what are now the southern states of Mexico. The Olmecs had their own writing system and calendar. Little is known, however, of Mexico's first great culture, including what name they gave themselves. The word Olmec is of a later origin and means "inhabitant of the rubber country." The area of Mexico where they flourished—the states of Veracruz and Tabasco—is extremely humid and dissolved the human remains of these ancient inhabitants, so it remains unknown what they looked like. Famously, this civilization left, among other things, the gigantic Olmec heads that, for centuries, were hidden in the jungle until they were discovered in the mid-19th century. The physical features of these heads, which presumably represent the Olmecs, continues to attract the attention of anthropologists for their obvious African features, with their round head, oblique eyes, short and wide nose, and thick lips. The proposal that the Olmecs were migrants from sub-Saharan Africa, or that at least the culture had contact with ancient sailors from the so-called Dark Continent, although fanciful, has not been completely dismissed. The Olmecs, who erected several cities, eventually scattered in the jungle around 100 BCE and eventually assimilated into other groups.

Two Empires

With the change of the era, at a time when Christianity was spreading in the Middle East and Turkey, the first cities flourished in the center of Mexico, along with other aspects that accompany the birth of a civilization: a political system, hieroglyphic writing, palaces, markets, a bureaucracy, and armies.

The city of Teotihuacan, a word that means "the place where the gods dwell," was the first metropolis in North America, founded in 300 BCE. Its impressive pyramids are preserved today in the vicinity of Mexico City. According to a legend that the later Aztecs preserved, the gods gathered in Teotihuacan to create the moon, the sun, and the other celestial bodies. At its time of splendor, the city had more than one hundred thousand inhabitants, which was a smaller population but still similar to great cities like Alexandria, Ephesus, Carthage, and Antioch, making it one of the ten most populated cities in the world at the time. But certainly in those other cities of Asia and Africa, which at the moment were buoyant centers of Christianity, people would have been horrified to see the public rituals that were carried out in the form of human sacrifices and other ceremonies for the gods at the top of the great pyramids of the sun and the moon. These rites continued for many centuries.

Teotihuacan dominated central Mexico without rivals. The priests, warriors, merchants, and artisans were the basis of its power. All houses had drainage systems and a central courtyard. Its inhabitants lived in that place until the 9th century CE. The culture of Teotihuacan was transmitted with such impetus to later civilizations that even centuries after the metropolis was abandoned, the inhabitants of ancient Mexico still made pilgrimages to seek the favor of gods like Tlaloc (the god of water) and especially Quetzalcoatl, the god of wind and air (similar to how Yahweh was for the ancient Hebrews, a storm god). Quetzalcoatl was represented by a feathered serpent. This god, whose first record of worship comes from the 1st century CE in Teotihuacan, eventually acquired messianic characteristics, and the Spanish conquerors associated it with the figure of Jesus Christ or with Thomas the Apostle.

Quetzalcoatl, the god of the wind, the morning star (Venus), the deity who stole corn to give it to men, the entity that sprayed the bones in the realm of the dead with blood in order to give life to humans, was also a person with a story, possibly a historical character that became merged with the god. His name was Ce-acatl Topiltizin, and he was a priest who had been conceived miraculously when his mother swallowed a precious stone. A virtuous and beloved man, he taught people the secrets of life and heaven and was deceived by an antagonistic witch who got him drunk and killed his followers. Quetzalcoatl fled and disappeared into the sea, where he promised that one day he would return to claim his own. Spanish sources fed by Native American informants refer to him as a divine man who wore a white robe and banned human sacrifice. Not surprisingly, the Spanish priests thought that the Mexica (the so-called "Aztecs" by later scholars) were talking about an apostle or perhaps Jesus himself. In fact, although it is not an official doctrine of the Mormons, some sectors of this church have tried to associate, even to this date, the figure of this ancient priest with that of the historical Jesus.

It is not so clear, however, as it was previously believed, if the Aztecs or Mexica were waiting for the return of Quetzalcoatl when the Spanish conquerors made their arrival and if the city gates were opened to the invaders because the Native Americans thought the

Spaniards were Quetzalcoatl's appointed. The version that Montezuma stepped aside and handed over his throne to Hernán Cortés when he saw him is most likely a fictional story created by Cortés in order to justify his actions. Today, prominent historians concede that these two myths—the Spaniards as gods, and the submissive surrender of Montezuma—are an invention of the conquerors *after the city's fall.* Just a few years after the destruction of Tenochtitlan, there was already evidence of the myth of Cortés as Quetzalcoatl. Anthropologists have found images of Quetzalcoatl in almost all of Mexico's current territory, from Sinaloa in the northwest to the south, which shows that at the time of the meeting of the two cultures, its mythology was already disseminated throughout the region.

Around the same time as Teotihuacan dominated the central plateau, the Mayas flourished on the Yucatan Peninsula, and they were perhaps the earliest advanced civilization on the American continent. From the 19th century onward, their history, ceremonial centers, cyclical calendar, mathematics, and writings generated fascination among anthropologists. The Mayas were captivated with the universe, including its time and measures. In their observatories, they calculated the duration of the year and the motion of Venus. They also discovered the existence of planets moving over the background of motionless stars, invented constellations, recorded eclipses, and established the existence of great cosmic cycles to measure the passage of time, from one year to a 400-year cycle until reaching the major time span, the so-called "Alautun," whose duration was millions of years. The exact duration of their eras is not known since there are currently discrepancies in the interpretation.

At first, it was believed that the Maya of Yucatan had formed a harmonious empire dedicated to mathematics, observing the stars, and building impressive monuments that survive to this day, but this idea has now been abandoned, especially after the discovery of the murals of Bonampak, the most extensive conserved of that culture.

Now we know that the Mayan kingdoms lived in a state of permanent warfare with each other. The city of Chichen Itza, the last great Mayan city to emerge in the jungle, left an impressive pyramid of 365 steps, one for each day of the year, the largest ballgame in the Americas, an astronomical observatory, and skull altars.

In southern Mexico, Monte Albán (in the modern state of Oaxaca), founded on top of a mountain, came to dominate a huge area and had artisans in Teotihuacan. Its residents worshiped more than forty gods. At the beginning of the 6th century, two great cultures, the Maya and Teotihuacan, coexisted on both extremes of the land and established commercial relations, thus extending their influence, their language, their gods, and their architecture to the entire central region of the country we now call Mexico.

The First Mexico

"At the edge of the cave they saw an erect eagle on the cactus devouring happily, tearing things apart when eating, and so [when] the eagle saw them, it ducked very much its head."

—*Mexicayotl Chronicle*, 16th century

But the most representative civilization of ancient Mexico, in fact the most important and authentic expression of "empire" on the American continent, was the Mexica or Aztec civilization, whose importance was so great that its symbols, name, and even culture persist in the country. The leaders of modern Mexico have dug through the history and culture of the Aztecs in search of motifs for the creation of a national identity. The word "Aztec," though, is of modern origin. The inhabitants of ancient Mexico would have preferred to call themselves "Mexica," and they were a part of a larger group called the Nahua, whose language was Nahuatl, the lingua franca of the time. Many words in Nahuatl survive in the Spanish spoken in Mexico today. For example, the Spanish language assimilated words like "cocoa," "chili," "coyote," "tomato," "guacamole," and "chocolate," among many others. When the Aztec Empire arose in central Mexico, not far from the place where the great city of Teotihuacan and its pyramids once stood, the great civilizations of the classical period had already dissolved. Teotihuacan had been abandoned, with the reasons for its sudden disappearance still unclear. In Yucatan, the populous Mayan cities had been swallowed by the jungle.

The Mexica, a migrant group from northern Mexico, reached what is now Mexico City around 1325 CE, following the prophecy of one of their gods. On their pilgrimage, they stopped in the sacred and abandoned city of Teotihuacan to ask for divine guidance. Their arrival in the Valley of Mexico was not easy. They were attacked by the peoples already established there, who expelled them from their countries. Exhausted, and without resources, the Mexica were surrounded by hostile cities and confined to inhospitable places. Persecuted to the shore of the great lake of Texcoco, the Mexica built rafts and entered the waters to save their lives. There, they hid among the reeds, islets, and swampy lands, among the aquatic vegetation of Texcoco, where they remade their forces and fled once again. Across the lake, going from side to side, according to the story that Dominican Friar Diego Durán collected years later, they saw the sign that their god Huitzilopochtli had given them so that they would know the place where they should settle, their promised land or, more exactly, their promised *water*–an eagle on top of a cactus. Thus, the people that had roamed for so long ended its exodus of more than two hundred years with the installation of the first stone of their temple on the lake. This narrative, the "official" story that the Aztecs told the Europeans, might be idealized. When the Mexica passed from a small subdued human group to the greatest empire of pre-Hispanic Mexico, they burned the previous accounts and wrote a new history where they were the ones chosen to rule the world.

What is indisputable is that over time, the humble aquatic settlement became one of the largest cities in the world. There, they built their capital on an islet in the middle of a lake. It seems that the piece of land where the Aztecs built their very first village was called

"Mexico," meaning "in the center of the moon lake." The whole city was named Tenochtitlan. Those insignificant islets and their surroundings were spaces with abundant fishing, hunting, and gathering, meaning it was an ideal place to settle. Their position in the middle of a lake also gave them a strategic advantage: avoiding friction with neighboring cities, which were involved in unceasing expansionist wars. The lack of defined physical boundaries facilitated neutrality and concrete agreements and alliances. Thus, an insignificant hamlet became a metropolis in a few decades.

At this time, there emerged a philosophy of war that was closely linked to the cosmos, the idea that continuous human sacrifices were necessary to help the sun in its daily struggle against the forces of darkness and to sustain the battle of the eagle and tiger knights on behalf of the uninterrupted movement of stars and planets. In the archaeological record, representations of human sacrifices began to multiply at this time. But not everything was barbarism and cruelty. At the same time, the arts and education flourished; the Aztec, or Mexica, created sculptures, paintings, and other works; in the apogee of the Aztec Empire, more than sixty thousand canoes converged every day in the city of Tenochtitlan, which was supported on piles and trunks in the style of Venice and was larger than any European capital of the 15th century.

The inhabitants of Tenochtitlan planted crops on firm land and also on floating islands called *chinampas*, which were supported with piles. There were up to a thousand people in charge of cleaning the streets, which were swept every day, and the garbage was incinerated in huge fires that brightened the streets at night. Since Texcoco was a salty lake, there were also canals or aqueducts that carried water from nearby springs for a population that, it is worth mentioning, was neat and clean as in modern standards, and who enjoyed taking a daily bath.

Their economic, political, and social organization reached a very high level. In the nearby Tlatelolco market—which still persists in some form today—up to fifty thousand people gathered on market days. In Tlatelolco, people bought and sold with the local currency (cocoa beans), and the city was adorned by temples, palaces, and statues in the streets, squares, and other important points. When the first Europeans saw Tenochtitlan, a city greater than any of those in Europe, suddenly appearing in the misty valley, floating on a lake surrounded by snowy volcanoes, they wondered if they were seeing visions. An advanced civilization that had flourished independently of the Old World was in front of their very eyes.

One of those first witnesses, the Spaniard Hernán Cortés, left a valuable description of the great city, a kind of American Venice divided in four quarters separated by four avenues that radiated from the center and crossed by canals where people traveled in canoes that went from one place to another. Cortés wrote:

This great city of Temixtitan [sic] is situated in this salt lake, and from the main land to the denser parts of it, by whichever route one chooses to enter, the distance is two leagues. There are four avenues or entrances to the city, all of which are formed by artificial causeways, two spears' length in width. The city is as large as Seville or Cordoba; its streets, I speak of the principal ones, are very wide and straight; some of these, and all the inferior ones, are half land and half water, and are navigated by canoes. All the streets at intervals have openings, through which the water flows, crossing from one street to another; and at these openings, some of which are very wide, there are also very wide bridges, composed of large pieces of timber, of great strength and well put together; on many of these bridges ten horses can go abreast.

Cortés and his companions were amazed at the commercial activity that took place in Tenochtitlan and the neighboring Tlatelolco. Cortés wrote in his letters, or "relations," to Spain that the city had many public squares, where markets and other places for buying and selling items were situated. A particular square, according to the conqueror, was twice the size of Salamanca (located in Spain) and completely surrounded by porticoes, where every day, more than sixty thousand people gathered to trade—a city in itself. "All kinds of merchandise that the world affords [are found], embracing the necessaries of life, as for instance articles of food, as well as jewels of gold and silver, lead, brass, copper, tin, precious stones, bones, shells, snails, and feathers."

The city had an herb street, where people bought an infinite variety of roots and medicinal herbs (which, to this day, Mexicans are still very fond of). There were barbershops where people cut their hair or went just to wash it, as well as many stores where food and drinks were consumed—in other words, the predecessors of modern restaurants. "The way of living among the people," Cortés wrote, incredulous that such a civilization could exist outside the Christian world, "is very similar to that of Spain, and considering that this is a barbarian nation, separated from the knowledge of the true God or the communication with enlightened nations, one may well marvel at the order and good governance that is maintained wherever it may be."

This was the city of Mexico in the first decades of the 16th century. But a traumatic event, which would forever transform the face of the region and the entire continent, would cause the Aztecs to lose everything in an ear-splitting collapse. Their city, their culture, their families, and their own nation would suddenly come to an end. That curse came floating by the sea on Good Friday, April 22nd, 1519.

Chapter 2 – The Spanish-Aztec War and New Spain

"The invaders saw things never seen or ever dreamed of."

—*Mexicayotl Chronicle*

"When we gazed upon all this splendour at once, we scarcely knew what to think, and we doubted whether all that we beheld was real. A series of large towns stretched themselves along the banks of the lake, out of which still larger ones rose magnificently above the waters. Innumerable crowds of canoes were plying everywhere around us; at regular distances we continually passed over new bridges, and before us lay the great city of Mexico in all its splendour."

—Bernal Díaz

In 1519, while an expedition commanded by Hernán Cortés touched the Yucatan Peninsula, 1,300 kilometers (almost 808 miles) away, in what is now the historic center of Mexico City, Emperor Montezuma II, the ninth king of the Aztecs, ruled a vast territory that comprised the entire southern half of Mexico. These lands were brimming with peoples subjected to the Aztecs and who were resentful of the intolerable tributes, including humans necessary for the sacrifices to placate the gods. From the steps of the main temple of Tenochtitlan, the blood of those sacrificed to the gods descended like rivers.

The Aztecs believed that once a victim was sacrificed, their blood was carried by eagles, allowing the cosmos to maintain its order and the sun to rise every morning. The myths of salvation were adapted to military interests: those who died in war went to the sky of the sun led by Teoyaomiqui, a goddess who wore a necklace made of hearts, hands, and skulls, and whose head was Death itself. Sometimes Teoyaomiqui was represented as being decapitated, and from her neck sprouted streams of blood in the form of snakes. The bodies of women who died in their first birth became sacred, and the young soldiers tried to steal parts of them, especially the hair and fingers, to make talismans that hung from their shields. The children who died at the age of breastfeeding went to a place where there was a tree whose branches dripped milk, those who died from causes related to water went to a place where everything existed in abundance, and those who died a natural death were not rewarded or punished because they had simply fulfilled their destiny.

Some scholars have estimated that the Aztecs sacrificed more than two hundred thousand people per year, and on the days of the reconsecration of the great pyramid of Tenochtitlan, there was an average of fifteen human sacrifices per minute. It was from that splendid and bloody center of the Aztec Empire that Montezuma extended trade routes to Panama. Several indigenous peoples—the Tlaxcalans, the Huastecos, the Totonacs, and many more, who produced an abundance of corn, cocoa, vanilla, fruits, cotton, and precious woods—received visits from tax collectors and paid tributes that were hateful to them. Although they occasionally rebelled, fed up with the Aztec domain, they were firmly subdued by the Triple Alliance, which had Tenochtitlan at its head. The Mayan peoples, who were past their time of splendor, were too far away and not organized but fragmented in many small kingdoms throughout the

Yucatan Peninsula. During his reign, Montezuma also raised the demands in the education of the youth, but like all Aztec emperors, who were faithful servants of the god of war, Huitzilopochtli, Montezuma sat on his throne under a kind of black cloud, a kind of fatalism about an uncertain future envisioned by the astrologers of his court.

The Meeting

Montezuma was 45 when a Spanish vessel shipwrecked on its way from Panama to the island of Santo Domingo, located in the Antilles Sea. It was the year 1511. The sailors drifted for several days until they saw some unknown beaches, which, at first, they thought was yet another island. Without knowing it, they would become the first Spaniards to put their foot on the American mainland, a continent hitherto unknown to European navigators. When they entered what is now Yucatan in search of supplies, they were attacked by the Mayas. Although almost all of them died, at least two managed to save their lives, a sailor named Jerónimo de Aguilar and another named Gonzalo Guerrero. Two years later, Hernán Cortés arrived on the island of Cozumel, where he heard that a couple of Spanish shipwrecks lived there, and he went to rescue them.

When he found his fellow countryman Jerónimo de Aguilar, he did not recognize him; after eight years, he had lost his fluency in Spanish, he was dressed as a Mayan, and his skin was brown. But Aguilar knew the language of the Yucatec people, and Cortés knew that was going to be of great advantage to him, and indeed, he later employed Aguilar as an interpreter.

Aguilar recognized the Spanish ships and went to look for his shipwrecked companion Gonzalo Guerrero, who lived in another village. But his comrade of adversity refused to go with the expedition. His words were kept in the annals of the soldier and chronicler Bernal Díaz: "Brother, I am married and have three kids. Go with God, that I have my face carved and my eyebrows pierced [in the Mayan style]. And you see these my little children, how beautiful they are!" Guerrero was so esteemed in his town that he had been designated captain in times of war. He was also, namely, the father of the first modern Mexican, that is, the offspring of a European man and a Native American woman. Aguilar tried to talk his partner into joining the expedition, telling him that if he so desired, he could take his children with him. Guerrero's wife, a Mayan woman, rebuked Aguilar and asked him to leave. Nothing could change Guerrero's mind, who lived among the Mayas until the end of his life. He died, ironically, fighting against the Spaniards.

The next decisive meeting of Cortés occurred days later when, in March of 1519, he arrived at the modern state of Tabasco, on the coast of the Gulf of Mexico, on his way south. There, he received from a native lord a group of twenty young female slaves that Cortés distributed among his men. A remarkable woman of about nineteen to twenty years old was in that group—her birthdate can only be approximated. She was called Malinalli. Malinalli had a sad story to tell. Her father had married for the second time and sold her as a slave to some merchants, who, in turn, handed her over to a chief in Tabasco who met Cortés on his way to Tenochtitlan. Jerónimo de Aguilar, the castaway rescued in Yucatan, noted that young Malinalli, who according to oral tradition was beautiful and cultured, spoke the Mayan language and another tongue he couldn´t understand, which was Nahuatl. Since Malinalli could communicate with Aguilar, an efficient combination of interpreters was thus formed: Cortés spoke in Spanish with Aguilar, Aguilar spoke in Mayan with Malinalli, and then she translated the message in Nahuatl for the Native Americans. In this way, Cortés was able to communicate with Emperor Montezuma. In command of 518 soldiers, 110 sailors, 16 horse riders, 32 crossbowmen, 13 gunmen, ten cannons, and four falconets, Cortés took the young woman for himself and made her his faithful companion, lover, and confidant. Devoted and supportive, Malinalli was at his side through all of the hazards and decisive moments of the conquest of the Aztec Empire. The young woman called Malinalli, who was baptized as Marina by the

Spaniards and later known as Malinche by the Mexicans, is to date, due to her proximity to the invaders, one of the most controversial women in the history of Mexico. There is even a word derived from her name to refer to excessive love for all things foreign and the betrayal of one's own: Malinchism.

A month after these events, on April 21st, 1519, Cortés and his eleven ships touched the coast of Veracruz. There, Cortés founded the first city in continental America: Villa Rica de la Veracruz, one of the most important ports today. Along the way, two unexpected developments happened that encouraged the expedition to move inland: the chiefs and *caciques* (minor local bosses) that Cortés was finding were offering him alliances since they wanted to free themselves from Montezuma, and they provided him with valuable information on what he would find inland. The other surprise was the arrival of the first ambassadors of Montezuma, who had traveled to the Gulf of Mexico to meet Cortés; they had gifts, which consisted of much gold, and encouraged him to turn around and leave. The strategy had the opposite effect, as they only aroused Cortés's interest and the greed of his men. When the Spanish expedition finally went up and down the mountains and saw the city on the lake in the distance, it was the month of November 1519. They gazed in awe at the pyramids, water canals, which were full of canoes, gardens, and thousands of men, women, and children. They were speechless, "gazing on such wonderful sights, we did not know what to say, or whether what appeared before us was real," wrote Bernal Díaz years later, remembering everything he had seen and heard.

When Cortés entered Tenochtitlan and met the monarch, the king of the largest city on the continent, both men bowed deeply to each other or exchanged necklaces, or Cortés tried to hold him in the European style, and then two lords stopped him from touching Montezuma. The accounts vary. Nonetheless, the meeting was friendly but tense. Both sides displayed their diplomatic skills, but the clash of cultures was imminent. For the moment, both men could communicate with each other thanks to Malinalli, the young indigenous woman who had stood by Cortés's side since Tabasco and understood the emperor's language. Malinalli was probably the most astonished of all, being in front of that powerful lord she had only heard rumors of.

Montezuma took Cortés to some spacious rooms and then returned with gold, silver, feathers, and other gifts. It was an important moment not only in the history of Mexico but of humanity: the meeting between Montezuma and Hernán Cortés in the place where Mexico City stands today symbolizes the moment when humanity and civilization, which, in the beginning, moved east and west from the Fertile Crescent, came full circle and found itself again. It was one of the most important meetings of human history. That day, the earth became a global village. The idea that the natives saw the Spaniards as gods and that they knelt before them, or that they saw Quetzalcoatl in Cortés, are later developments, a part of the victors' propaganda and excuses of the defeated. There is no evidence in Aztec history prior to this encounter that Montezuma was really waiting for the return of the god. On the contrary, the encounter seems to have been between two equally proud and confident forces. And it is even possible that Emperor Montezuma was actually in full control of the situation, planning to put his newest acquisitions in cages or ritually sacrifice them.

For months, life between visitors and locals was cordial, but things were boiling beneath the surface. Cortés, suspicious all the time, feared for his safety, and finally, fearing a betrayal, he arrested Montezuma. Since the search for allies was one of the routine procedures of the Spaniards in conquest wars, Cortés took advantage of the hostility of the many people who were against the Aztecs and formed alliances to conquer Tenochtitlan. Several indigenous kingdoms shared his purpose: to see Montezuma's fall. It was not, as has been said many times before, a handful of brave Spanish adventurers or Cortés's genius that conquered the vast empire;

rather, it was a situation more similar to a civil war or, more precisely, a rebellion of all the subjugated peoples against the Triple Alliance. The Aztec Empire was, in many ways, conquered by other Native Americans.

The hostilities began when Cortés was absent from the city for a few days. One of his captains committed a massacre against the civilian population that was celebrating in the Templo Mayor. The furious Mexica rebelled en masse. The most widespread version is that Emperor Montezuma died during this episode when Cortés returned to Tenochtitlan and asked him to go out and talk to his countrymen, appealing them to retreat. But his bellicose citizens supposedly stoned him. However, both this incident, as with others related to the conquest of Mexico, should be taken with a grain of salt as possible inventions of Europeans to blame the incident on the Aztec people and not on the Spaniards. The Montezuma Codex, which is preserved in the National Library of Anthropology and History of Mexico, is a fragmentary amate codex of the 16th century that contains people and historical scenes with texts written in Nahuatl in Latin characters. There is a drawing of Montezuma with a rope tied to his neck held by a Spaniard. Beside this scene is a stabbed Native American. Above one can see the Templo Mayor of Tenochtitlan burning in flames. At the top is Cortés on horseback. The codex shows, it seems, the major events of the siege of Tenochtitlan, including the destruction of the city and the killing of Montezuma by the Spaniards.

After the massacre at the Templo Mayor, Cortés and his men suffered a devastating defeat and were expelled from Tenochtitlan. They were almost annihilated. At this point, history could have changed, but the Aztecs inexplicably did not follow them to exterminate them. Once he was free from harm, Cortés, shattered, sat down to cry under a tree, an incident known as "The Tragic Night." The tree where Cortés shed bitter tears still exists in Mexico City, although it is very deteriorated after an intentional fire in 1980.

The Aztecs lost their chance to liquidate the invaders due to the arrival of a new and much more ruthless enemy: smallpox.

With the help of nearly 200,000 Native American allies, peoples who were conquered by the Aztecs, Cortés regained his strength and put Tenochtitlan under siege. Like all historic sieges, this one was prolonged and cruel. Cortés cut off the water supply, and virtually all the peoples of the region, who had been oppressed for over a hundred years and forced to contribute their share of men and women for human sacrifice, supported the Europeans, meaning no one was coming to Tenochtitlan's aid. When Tenochtitlan fell, more than forty thousand bodies were floating on Lake Texcoco. The enemies of the Aztecs showed no mercy, and the events that took place after the city's fall practically amounted to genocide. Within a couple of years of Cortés's arrival, and without going through a phase of decline like other empires, the most powerful ruler that had existed in Mexico was dead, his body thrown in the lake, his great city lying in ruins.

A Supreme Case of Syncretism

When the Spaniards arrived at the great Tenochtitlan, the heart of the Aztec Empire, Emperor Montezuma II was allied with two other kingdoms, Texcoco and Tlacopan, known as the Triple Alliance. The confederation dominated the southern half of modern Mexico, from the Pacific to the Gulf shores. The progressive conquests of these territories gave Europeans access to the Pacific Ocean and, what Columbus had intended in the first place three decades before, a coveted route to the Far East. In the next century, marching from Tenochtitlan to the north, the Spanish captains would absorb more portions of the territory, as far away as California and Texas, with the unexpected "help" of the most effective biological weapon: germs.

The diseases of Europe, which were unknown in America, traveled faster than the Spanish expeditions. As the 16th century progressed, the new viceroyalty and the future Mexican Republic would be known as New Spain, a colossal territory that spread from

Mexico City to Oregon and Central America. Little has been said about the role of African slaves in the Spanish-Aztec war. As early as 1537, just fifteen years after the fall of Tenochtitlan, there were ten thousand Africans in Mexico, some of whom briefly rebelled and appointed a black king. However, his royal dream was ephemeral—after a few days of wearing his crown, he was captured and publicly executed.

The indigenous cultures did not fade away into oblivion with the Spanish occupation. One of the most characteristic symbols of Mexico, the image of the Virgin of Guadalupe, with both its indigenous and European elements, has its dark origins in the first years immediately after the fall of Tenochtitlan when there were still ruins and people who remembered the lake red with the blood of the dead. The tradition says that in 1531, the Virgin Mary appeared to a Native American named Juan Diego in the surroundings of Mexico City, on the slopes of a hill where there was previously a temple dedicated to Tonantzin, the mother of the gods. There, the Native Americans made offerings and came from faraway lands with presents. Juan Diego was a survivor of one of the most violent cultural confrontations in the history of mankind. A poem composed in those years by the survivors said, "And all this happened to us. We saw it, we observed it. With this mournful and sad fate we found ourselves in anguish. On the roads lie broken arrows, the hairs are scattered. The houses are roofless, their walls are blood-red." It was in this context of colossal loss that the image of Guadalupe emerged.

According to the legend, the Virgin told Juan Diego during her first appearance to go to Bishop Zumárraga and ask him to build a temple for her on that site. In one of the oldest chronicles written in Nahuatl, the Virgin Mary says:

I want very much that they build my sacred little house here...because I am truly your compassionate mother, yours and of all the people who live together in this land, and of all the other people of different ancestries, those who love me, those who cry to me, those who seek me, those who trust in me, because there I will listen to their weeping, their sadness, to remedy, to cleanse and nurse all their different troubles, their miseries, their suffering.

Juan Diego ignored the identity of that "beloved maiden," and he went to the bishop to tell him what he had seen on the hill. The priest did not believe him. In the third and last apparition, the image of the Virgin Mary became adhered to the *tilma* of the humble Native American as a proof for the bishop, and this same piece of cloth is still venerated today in the Basilica of Guadalupe in Mexico City, which is the most visited Catholic sanctuary in the world after the Vatican. It would not be an exaggeration to say that the image of Guadalupe—whose cult rapidly spread among Native Americans and Spaniards—was the first element of a union, which eventually transformed into a nation.

Historical fact or pious legend, most Mexicans do not take the story lightly. Until recently, a saying circulated in Mexico that said there were only two things that were untouchable: the president and the Virgin of Guadalupe. Most historians believe that the story was invented by the Franciscans. Anthropologists point out that stories do not come from nothing and that a historical core must lie behind the embellished legend. What no one questions is that the Virgin of Guadalupe has been the most important religious and political symbol in Mexico's history, a kind of unofficial flag. Its influence has extended even to the Mexican diaspora, where it is a sign of identity, pride, and struggle among undocumented immigrants in the United States. For Mexicans, it is not necessary to be religious to believe in the power of the Virgin of Guadalupe as a representative of Mexicanness and as a banner of their most important struggles, as will be seen later.

Another Colonial Jewel: Chapultepec Castle

From the colonial era comes another of Mexico City's most distinctive icons: the Castle of Chapultepec, which is, to date, the only genuine castle in the Americas, then located in the outskirts of

Mexico City. In 1783, Viceroy Matías de Gálvez, who is fondly remembered for his love for the Native Americans, came up with the idea of building a new palace for the transfer of powers among viceroys. Viceroy Gálvez died suddenly without seeing his dream come true, but he had sown the idea. It would fall upon his son Bernardo to complete the castle. Bernardo Gálvez was an experienced soldier who was a key ally of the American Revolution—the city of Galveston, Texas, is named after him—and had great sympathy for the Mexican people. He was so popular among the Mexicans that the Spanish Crown distrusted him. The first stone for the castle was laid on November 23rd, 1785. It is intriguing to think that the intention behind Chapultepec could have been more than pure ostentation. It's probable that it was built exactly for the purpose that castles had been constructed in Europe: for military purposes, and in Mexico's case, in order to pave the way to independence.

Ideas of liberty were already running throughout the Americas, and Gálvez had a distinguished military career with many triumphs. People began frequently speaking about the building as a fortress, and there was a rumor that Gálvez had been thinking of declaring the independence of Mexico and installing his palace in Chapultepec, according to the traveler and geographer Alexander von Humboldt, who visited New Spain in 1804. If that was indeed the case, then the king of Spain was not so wrong to harbor suspicions and order the interruption of the castle's construction the following year. The beloved Viceroy Gálvez died in 1786, and Chapultepec was abandoned for many years. But a lot of history was going to happen on that hill in the following two centuries.

Chapter 3 – The Birth of a Nation

"All former Spanish colonies are now in insurrection. What kind of government will they establish? How much liberty can they bear without intoxication? Are their chiefs sufficiently enlightened to form a well-guarded government, and their people to watch their chiefs? Have they mind enough to place their domesticated Indians on a footing with the whites?"

—Thomas Jefferson to Alexander von Humboldt in April 1811

The colonial era under the dominion of the Spanish Empire lasted for three centuries. Between 1521, when Tenochtitlan capitulated, and 1821, when Mexico signed its act of independence, New Spain increased its power from Lake Texcoco in every geographical direction to form a colossal country of almost five million square kilometers. The Spaniards, hoping to find gold and silver, went north and south, conquering and subjugating peoples until they reached as far as Panama in the south and the center of the United States in the north. The stories about El Dorado, a city made of gold, and the Fountain of Youth, tales that were propagated by the Spaniards, encouraged more expeditions in search of mythical kingdoms. Only the unruly peninsula of Yucatan and the Mayas remained in constant insurrection for centuries, composing an impenetrable and fiercely independent zone.

The Kingdom of New Spain, part of the Habsburg Empire, came to include modern-day Mexico, the American states of California, Nevada, Colorado, Utah, New Mexico, Arizona, Texas, Oregon, Washington, Florida, and parts of Idaho, Montana, Wyoming, Kansas, Oklahoma, Alabama, Mississippi, and Louisiana. It also included the modern countries of Central America, the Philippines, Guam, and other islands. However, like everything in the American continent at the time, these borders were unstable. The Spanish conquests responded—besides the crave for gold—to France's expansionism in the east and Russia in the west, which led Spain to populate the Pacific Coast up to California with missions and towns.

During the colonial period, a very high mortality rate due to European diseases, forced labor, and war resulted in a real catastrophe for the native population. When Cortés met Montezuma, the land that would become New Spain had a population of about twenty million inhabitants; in three centuries, this figure dropped to six million. On the other hand, with the arrival of more Spaniards to America, including women, the European and the indigenous population intermarried and formed the mestizo population, which predominates to this day in Mexico, although it should be mentioned that Native Americans, such as the Maya and the northern tribes, resisted assimilation. This is the reason why Mexico still has some of its original population. In the last years of New Spain, a census ordered by Viceroy Revillagigedo revealed that there were 60 percent indigenous, 22 percent mestizos, 18 percent white, and a minimal number of African Americans. The whites—including the clergy—owned almost all property.

Although libertarian ideas were already running throughout New Spain, it was not until 1810 that a priest named Miguel Hidalgo managed to gather a crowd early in the morning of September in a small village in central Mexico. Armed with sticks, hoes, and a few rusty guns, people started a revolution that would last, with intermittence, more than a decade. His first pronouncements were against political and economic subordination. "My friends and compatriots," Hidalgo shouted, "there is no longer for us neither king nor taxes; this shameful gavel, which only suits slaves, we have endured for three centuries as a sign of tyranny and servitude; a terrible stain that we will know how to wash with our struggle. The time has come for our emancipation; the hour of our freedom has sounded; and if you know its great value, you will help me defend it from the ambitious grip of tyrants." But the first revolutionaries were not actually seeking total independence from Spain. They were rebelling against Napoleon's occupation of Spain. Or at least that was their alibi.

Before Father Hidalgo, there had been sporadic Native American rebellions, African slave riots, miners' strikes, and protests over hunger. On more than one occasion, the battle cry "Death to the bad government!" had been voiced. The column that followed Father Hidalgo, which was more similar to an angry, murderous mob than a true army, carried a banner that can be considered Mexico's first flag: a representation of the Virgin of Guadalupe, an image venerated in Mexico City shortly after the fall of Tenochtitlan, a symbol that Hidalgo knew appealed to all social classes and could attract everyone, Native Americans and whites. Hidalgo and his men captured a few minor cities. However, his ardent and apparently unstoppable rebellion was stifled by the superior Spanish forces after their first successes in central Mexico. It was too late, though, as Hidalgo's call echoed through all the land. Another priest named José María Morelos, a rude military man from the south, embraced the cause. Morelos was a brown-skinned, short, and stocky determined man, who always wore a headscarf moistened with medicinal herbs because he suffered from migraines.

The leaders of the independence movement proclaimed Morelos "Most Serene Highness"—a title that Father Hidalgo had adopted for himself— but the Morelos vehemently rejected it and preferred to be called "Servant of the Nation." This was more than politics or diplomacy. Morelos was a true revolutionary. When they showed him a draft of the constitution for the new nation, where the freedom of Mexico was stipulated but sovereignty still resided in the Spanish king, Fernando (Ferdinand) VII, Morelos raised his glass and exclaimed, "Long live Spain, but a sister Spain, not one dominating America." Morelos also got rid of the image of the Virgin as a flag for the insurgents and, for the first time, placed the image of an eagle on a cactus.

Morelos, unlike Hidalgo, was a true soldier. Upon learning of his military genius, Napoleon Bonaparte allegedly said, "Give me three Morelos and I will conquer the world." The skillful priest became the soul of the Mexican War of Independence. Among his innovations was the creation of a children's battalion that helped him in his most important battles. When under siege in Cuautla, a town in southern Mexico, the rebels fled, fearing the imminent attack. Only one boy named Narciso Mendoza stood still, facing the column charging against him. Mechanically, the twelve-year-old boy took a torch and lit up a loaded cannon with its mouth directed toward the street where the royalist column was coming. This unexpected and fearless action allowed the revolutionaries to return to their positions and restore order. Morelos assigned the boy a salary throughout the campaign.

In 1813, Morelos presented a document called *Feelings of the Nation*, a kind of proto-constitution for the new country. Morelos decreed the abolition of slavery and the elimination of the legal figure of the king of Spain; laws were also issued to eliminate poverty and limit wealth, jobs would be reserved for the Americans (this is, not for Europeans), and it decreed an end for the payment of tributes. As a form of government, unlike most of the leaders of the revolution, Morelos believed in a brand-new republic, free from its past. "It is lawful for a conquered kingdom to reconquer itself, and for an obedient kingdom it is lawful not to obey the king, when the king is oppressive in his laws."

By the middle of the 1810s, the independence revolution came to a stall. Both Hidalgo and Morelos had been arrested, tried by the Inquisition, declared heretics, excommunicated, and finally executed by the judicial authority. The new viceroy offered a pardon to the rebels, which many accepted, and by 1819, New Spain seemed to be at peace. A few minor *caudillos* (military or political leaders) barely survived in the mountains, but they continued the fight, and a few shots were heard here and there. One of those insurgents, Guadalupe Victoria, who would become the first president of Mexico, spent several years hiding in a cave. The revolution, weakened but with a spark of life, was left to Vicente Guerrero, a rebel from the south, who would become the second president of Mexico and the first African American president in the Americas. The viceroy of New Spain sent Guerrero's father to ask him, for the good of all, to surrender and accept the pardon. Guerrero received his father, listened to him, and then sent him away with a saying that people still remember: "*La Patria es primero*"— "The Motherland first." Things took a favorable turn as the new decade set in when the commander of the royalist forces of the south, Agustín de Iturbide, who was sent to crush Vicente Guerrero, instead became an ally. Together, they launched the Plan of Iguala, where they declared Mexico to be an independent, Catholic country and the home of Spaniards, Creoles (Mexican-born whites of Spanish heritage), Native Americans, blacks, and mestizos alike. With this alliance, the Spanish authorities realized that their cause was lost. Agustín de Iturbide marched into the capital on September 27th, 1821, and thus began the life of independent Mexico.

At this time, the name "Mexico" emerged to refer to the whole nation that would replace New Spain. During the colonial period, and since the times of the Spanish-Aztec war, the word Mexico appears in several documents but only in reference to Tenochtitlan and its sphere of influence. The whole territory was known as "America," "North America," "Mexican America" (in the first constitution), and "Anahuac" (pronounced *Anawak*), a name given by the Mexica to the world known to them. Anahuac means "the land completely surrounded by water" or, more formally, "the totality of what is between the waters." By Anahuac, they meant everything known between the Pacific and the Atlantic Oceans. The priest José María Morelos referred to the country as the Anahuac Republic. One of the most interesting references that anticipated the name that Mexico would adopt appeared in the *Texas Gazette* on May 25th, 1813, where it is called the "United States of Mexico." Finally, in 1816, the term "Mexican Republic" came up during the Mexican War of Independence to replace that of "New Spain." The flag of that republic, which did not exist yet except in the mind of the insurgents, was an eagle devouring a snake standing on a cactus in a lake. The country was embracing its indigenous past. The republic's official name became the "United Mexican States," which remains to this day. Although the whole world and its own inhabitants call it simply "Mexico," as of 2020, it is not yet the official name of the country.

Mexico declared itself independent in 1821, exactly three centuries later—minus one month—after the fall of Tenochtitlan. Spain lost all of its rights over New Spain, and Mexico began its own life as a monarchy. The annexation of the Captaincy General of Guatemala, which included all of Central America, was received gladly. The first emperor of Mexico was Agustín de Iturbide, and he was crowned on July 21st, 1822, inside the Cathedral of Mexico City in a remarkably original ceremony due to its novelty and the constitutional character of the ruler. It was an "inauguration, consecration and coronation" of a monarch, something unheard of; even more, Iturbide was also a "constitutional emperor." In the ceremony, which was meticulously prepared by the deputies in terms of symbolism and location of the attendees, Congress added several gestures to show that, contrary to Napoleon's, this would be a constitutional empire. It was Congress, not God, the pope, or a monarch, who put the crown on the emperor's head. Many saw the ceremony as a form of personal legitimation of Iturbide through the Church, but it actually was a somewhat different project, as Iturbide had not prepared the ritual. The members of Congress actually arranged the ceremony, and they were already positioning the legal body to be Iturbide's future rival.

Iturbide thus inherited a mammoth country that would have aroused the envy of Alexander the Great himself. From Panama in the south to the limits of Oregon in the north, it was almost five thousand miles from side to side, or five million square kilometers, which was greater than Alexander's empire. However, the only impressive thing about Mexico was its size: many territories were just wilderness and not much more. The task of building a country was just beginning, and for Mexico—which, since the first day, was divided into uncompromising factions—it would not be an easy task. In fact, in the following years, it would come close to disintegrating and dissolving. "I cannot imagine a worst punishment to Mexicans," said Spanish Mayor Miguel Bataller in the first years of the Mexican War of Independence, "than to let them govern themselves." The following decades apparently proved him right.

Chapter 4 – "From the Halls of Montezuma..."

"The insatiable ambition of the United States,

favored by our own weakness, caused that war."

Guillermo Prieto, 1847

Modern Mexico was born with problems. After eleven years of war, many parts of the country were in ruins; roads, buildings, and dams were destroyed, and the countryside was abandoned. The institutions had been dismantled, and two pressing problems would be the country's plague throughout the rest of the century: the bankruptcy of public finances and political divisions. The national treasury was empty, and future revenues were already committed. The empire of Agustín de Iturbide barely lasted a year before an internal rebellion deposed him. He was succeeded by Guadalupe Victoria—literally "Guadalupe Victory"—who became the first president. This was not his real name but one adopted in honor of the Virgin of Guadalupe and the victory over the Spaniards. Victoria, who had fought in the Mexican War of Independence, was succeeded by Vicente Guerrero, who was the first president of African American descent in the continent. Guerrero immediately decreed the liberation of black slaves and the permanent prohibition of slavery, which was a more symbolic gesture in central Mexico but one that would have acute repercussions in the north, where there were still slaves, specifically in Tejas (later Texas), which at that time was part of Mexico.

The government of Vicente Guerrero, the liberator of slaves, barely lasted for eight months before he was deposed by another rebellion. The third president could not achieve much either, as José María Bocanegra lasted for only one week. The next one, Anastasio Bustamante, was also deposed by a rebellion. This established a terrible precedent of what politics in Mexico would be like. Virtually all of the following presidents, until the end of the century, would be expelled by coups. That instability had immediate consequences on the territory that had once been New Spain. The first ones to say goodbye were the provinces of Central America (the modern countries of Guatemala, El Salvador, Honduras, Nicaragua, and Costa Rica). The state of Chiapas was next when it declared independence in 1823, then followed Yucatan.

The Republic of Yucatan

With Emperor Agustín de Iturbide gone, a rebel soldier named Antonio López de Santa Anna, a character who would give many headaches to Mexico in the following decades, tried to take the crown. However, instead of assuming the royal title of Antonio I as he wished, he was sent to be the governor of the farthest place in the country, Yucatan, the poorest state in the republic. It was almost equivalent to exile.

At that time, the only way to reach the peninsula, the home of the Maya and the old center of the pre-Columbian empire, was by sea. Far from Mexico City, Yucatan made a living off its commercial relations with the Caribbean—especially the vibrant city of Havana. Governor Santa Anna realized that the merchants and principal men in Yucatan felt closer to Spain than to Mexico as they even referred to Mexico as if it was another country. Yucatan's economy was supported by its trade with the Spanish colonies. The problem was that Mexico had ordered the governors to suspend trade with Spain and its colonies, including Cuba, which meant cutting off Yucatan's main source of income. The ruling class in the peninsula wanted to backpedal their independence and rejoin the Spanish Empire or, as a matter of choice, to declare itself a separate republic.

Santa Anna asked the federal government to lift the ban on trade with Cuba, but the central government frowned at the request. Santa Anna concluded—displaying his ability to think on a grand scale that he demonstrated his whole life—that the only way to help Yucatan would be to make Cuba independent and annex it to Mexico. With that purpose in mind, he would lead a liberating expedition. He assembled five thousand men and cleared the decks to leave in August 1824. According to his calculations, the inhabitants of the island would welcome him as a hero. However, Spain learned about his plans and fortified the island. Also, the government of Mexico, under diplomatic pressure from the United States and Great Britain, which did not wish to alter the balance in the Caribbean, pulled Santa Anna's ear. Without patronage or protection from anyone, what could have been an interesting chapter in Mexico's life was left aside.

Texas and the Alamo

Mexico extended for almost five million square kilometers but had only six million inhabitants, most of them crowding the south-center of the country. The nation's population density was 1.2 inhabitants per square kilometer, which was three times less than 19th-century Canada or Australia. It was practically an invitation to be invaded, and more regions began threatening to separate. The former New Spain, which had encompassed a territory superior to that of all of Western Europe, was facing the grim prospect of disintegrating. The separation of Central America had occurred without a single shot, and Yucatan was so far from everything that it was probably costlier to bring it into line than losing it.

Emperor Iturbide had been worried about distant Tejas since the beginning, as Spain had not made efforts to colonize it. Few people wanted, however, to move to Texas, although the government offered help to colonize its lands. There were good reasons for not wanting to take the family to Texas: the place was in the region of the Apaches, Comanches, Wichitas, Caddos, Tonkawas, Cherokees, and Karankawas, peoples that the Spanish had been unable to subdue. They were fierce, lionhearted warriors, stocked with horses and weapons. In 1835, the Mexican government intensified hostilities and even offered 100 pesos for each Apache scalp older than fourteen, 50 pesos for each woman's scalp, and 25 pesos per child.

In Tejas, the Mexican government donated land, granted tax exemptions, and allowed the free import of any item necessary for the colony. These were such exceptional conditions that US Secretary of State Henry Clay commented, "Little interest the Mexicans must have in keeping Texas, since they are giving it away!" In 1825, Stephen Austin arrived in the region after gaining the permission of the governor of Tejas, Antonio Martínez. Austin's first three hundred Anglo families came with their slaves. Mexico had granted them permission to enter on the condition that they swore allegiance to the country and brought no slaves, but Texas was too far away to enforce these laws. Not ten years had passed, and the Anglo-Saxon population—which consisted of well-educated, fairly well-off Protestants with an entrepreneurial, pioneering spirit—was three times larger than the Hispanics. Coexistence, unfortunately, was not amicable. Anglo-Saxon citizens (at that time, though, they were officially Mexicans) called Hispanics "greasers" because they thought their brown skin looked like dirt and because they fried their food in lard. It was also taboo for the Anglo-Saxon citizens to mix with Hispanic or mestizo families. Some began to see Mexicans as less than human and expendable, and the same went for Native Americans and blacks. Creed Taylor, a migrant who joined the Texas Revolution when he was fifteen, later recalled, "I thought I could shoot Mexicans just like Indians, or deer or turkeys, that's why I joined the war."

When Vicente Guerrero abolished slavery, the shockwaves came as an earthquake to Stephen Austin's colony, which already had eight thousand people. A quarter of them were black slaves. Being so distant, as Tejas was nine hundred miles away, there was little Mexico could do except increase its military presence and try to enforce the law. An 1830 report by an official envoy recommended the government suspend new entry permits, allow the arrival of citizens from Germany, Switzerland, and Mexico to curtail American influence, and finish the grace period without paying taxes. Austin's settlers began to conspire. In Mexico's capital, it was no longer a secret that conflict was brewing. When the Anglo-Saxons expelled the Hispanic Mexicans and declared themselves independent in 1836, Santa Anna, who first became president in 1833, left the presidential chair in a fury to go himself to crush the Texan separatists. When Santa Anna's troops arrived at El Alamo, an old fortress and mission built by the Spaniards in the 18th century, his men informed him that many Texan rebels had taken refuge there. According to some testimonies, the Mexican Army first sent a messenger with a white flag to offer the defenders an opportunity to surrender. Before the envoy could knock on the Alamo's door, William Travis, the man in charge, shot him. The act angered the Mexicans, who planted a red flag, meaning there would be no prisoners. The rebels had been declared as "pirates," and, therefore, deserved the death penalty. There were heavy casualties on both sides, who fought courageously. This dramatic clash, and the killing of prisoners in Fort Goliad, turned the Texas Revolution into a racial conflict. Santa Anna was captured days later when Sam Houston's soldiers surprised him in a poorly planned encampment, but instead of killing him, they took him to Houston, who made him a prisoner for several months.

The Texas Revolution is surrounded by folk tales and stories of heroism. One of the more colorful episodes, which does have a historical basis, although the details differ from one version to another, happened when General Santa Anna was a prisoner. One of the Texan soldiers saw him chewing a tree resin that the general was carrying among his belongings, and he asked what it was. Santa Anna replied that it was called chewing gum. The soldier, named Adams, remembered the information, and years later, he added sugar and colors and launched the multi-million dollar chewing gum industry alongside William Wrigley. Meanwhile, in Mexico, the military left Santa Anna alone as a prisoner of Houston. Eternally divided, the intrigues and betrayals in the capital resulted in Mexico losing the Provincia de Tejas, which proclaimed its independence in 1836 and became the Republic of Texas. Given that Chiapas and Yucatan eventually returned to the fold, the Lone Star State was the only one in Mexico that successfully separated through an armed revolt to become an independent country, although it did have the help of the United States.

Encouraged by Texas's example, the winds of independence once again blew in Yucatan, especially when Mexico decreed that the states would lose their sovereignty to become departments; their governors would be appointed in the capital and would lose their state militias. Yucatan took this occasion to separate for a second time. In retaliation, in 1841, the Mexican government blocked the ports of the peninsula. The governor of Yucatan symbolically ordered the removal of all the flags of Mexico and to raise the banner of the new republic. Yucatan's flag was vaguely reminiscent of the flag of the United States: a green field to symbolize independence, with red and white stripes, plus five stars representing the five divisions of the peninsula: Mérida, Izamal, Valladolid, Tekax, and Campeche.

Like Texas, Yucatan had an extensive coast in the Gulf of Mexico and thus had a direct connection with Texas by the sea without having to go inland. Therefore, both republics established relations and signed treaties of friendship and commerce. There was a diplomatic representation of Texas in Mérida and one of Yucatan in Austin. The president of Texas, Mirabeau B. Lamar, secretly negotiated an alliance against Mexico with Yucatan. For the Lone Star Republic, this was not just an altruistic move toward Yucatan: its own independent life was still fragile. While Mexico remained busy trying to suffocate the separatist attempts in the peninsula, it would leave Texas alone. Yucatan agreed to pay eight thousand dollars a month to Texas to defend the Yucatec coast from Mexican attacks, and both republics agreed that if there were any loot from the ships they captured, they would divide the spoils equally. Although Texan ships briefly patrolled the Yucatec coast, they never faced Mexico. However, isolated and endangered in the face of international and internal conflicts, a few years later, Yucatan recognized the need to rejoin Mexico and went back with its tail tucked between its metaphorical legs.

More urgent problems were brewing in the north. When the United States recognized Texas's independence, and a few years later even approved the annexation of the young republic, thus becoming the 28th state of the American Union, Mexico considered it a provocation. Despite the vehement recommendations of the British government, Mexican generals began to demand some kind of punishment. The words of the English proved to be prophetic. When Texas declared that the Rio Grande would be its new border, some 200 kilometers (a little over 124 miles) farther south than originally agreed, tensions broke out. The United States had previously offered to buy Texas and California from Mexico, but the latter had always refused. US President James K. Polk, an expansionist who had almost gone to war against Britain over Oregon, offered between twenty and forty million dollars for California and New Mexico. At the same time, Polk sent armed forces to the border, hoping to make a point, as well as hoping that Mexico would yield in the face of intimidation. In March of 1846,

American troops crossed the international border, which was marked by the Nueces River, and continued on until they reached the Rio Grande. This was a clear provocation since it was a region inhabited by Mexican families. When Mexico demanded them to withdraw, the first incident exploded. In Washington, DC, President Polk shouted from the rooftops that Mexico had shed American blood on American soil, which was false. With his goal accomplished, the US government quickly declared war against its weak southern neighbor.

The result of the Mexican-American War was predictable. At the beginning of the conflict, the United States had 22 million inhabitants, Mexico less than 7 million. The former had a buoyant economy and a powerful industrial base, while Mexico was bankrupt and, even in the midst of war, brimming with divisions. Instead of uniting against a common enemy, Mexicans continued with their eternal divisions and even planned more revolutions. Many state governors, mixing their priorities, refused to send troops to help with the war effort. Yucatan declared itself neutral, and others promoted rebellions against the presidents—incredibly, Mexico had seven presidents between 1846 and 1848, the years of war against the United States. The local chiefs left the federal government by itself, with obsolete weapons and improvised generals, to defend a huge semi-uninhabited territory against an industrial giant. The Mexican soldiers were mostly peasants recruited against their will, and they were poorly fed and demoralized to see how the wounded were abandoned on the battlefield. By January 1847, the United States had already annexed the Mexican provinces of New Mexico and California, as well as other parts of the country. The Texas Rangers, at this point in history famous for their indiscipline, and still seeking vengeance for the Alamo, massacred countless civilians in Monterrey.

This does not mean that Mexico did not fight to almost heroic levels with what little it had. In the middle of the war, the charismatic General Santa Anna returned. Exiled in Cuba, the former president learned about the military and political disaster in his country. Surprisingly, it was the Americans who went to ask for his help. Santa Anna received President Polk's envoy, a colonel named Alexander Atocha, who offered to ship him to Mexico with the promise that the United States would support him to be, once again, Mexico's president as long as he agreed to sell the desired territories to the US. Santa Anna gave the go-ahead. Believing that he had just created a traitor to his country and won an ally for the US, Polk sent a confidential letter to the commander of the US Gulf Squad, telling him to let Santa Anna pass unmolested if he tried to enter Mexico.

However, as soon as he set foot in Veracruz on September 12th, 1846, the US realized that Santa Anna had tricked them. A small crowd gathered to receive him as a hero as soon as they heard he was back. "Mexicans! There was a day when you greeted me with the title of Soldier of the People," Santa Anna addressed the group. "Let me take it again and devote myself even to the death in defense of the freedom and independence of the republic!" He quickly assembled an army from nowhere in San Luis Potosí and marched north to hold back General Zachary Taylor's unstoppable advance. On the outskirts of the city of Saltillo, the armies met. Santa Anna gave Taylor the chance to surrender. "Illustrious Sir," he wrote, "you are surrounded by 20,000 men and cannot in any human probability avoid suffering a rout, and being cut to pieces with your troops, but as you deserve consideration and particular esteem, I wish to save you from a catastrophe." When Taylor read the letter, he shouted, "Tell Santa Anna to go to hell! Put that in Spanish and send it to him!"

It was then that one of the fiercest battles of the Mexican-American War took place. Santa Anna, the one-legged soldier, emboldened his soldiers and rode like lightning among his troops. A testimony of the time pictured him this way:

He gallops from one position to another, despite the pain he suffers in his incomplete leg, indifferent to the grenades exploding around him. A horse falls dead and he falls to the ground, he stands up, takes another horse and continues running through the field with his sword drawn and waving only a small whip. Behind him, an aide-de-camp gallops to convey his orders. Soldiers are inspired by his example of courage, and during these hours of emotion, he reached perhaps the most honorable point of his career.

Incredibly, Santa Anna got a victory, but even more disconcerting to historians is the fact that after the heroic win, he withdrew from the battlefield, apparently because his troops could no longer go on. But the blunder was too much for the United States, which decided to open a second front in the Gulf of Mexico, where General Winfield Scott followed the route that three centuries earlier Cortés had taken toward the great Tenochtitlan. Scott began the attack on the capital in September 1847, which was the last line of resistance. At the gates of Mexico City, the church bells, which had been silent for days, rang like a siren. A dramatic and fierce battle ensued. Even the civilian population, who had been terrified as they hid in their houses, went outside or climbed to the rooftops to attack the invaders, including women and children. Mexico's government, which was now on the run, opened up the jails and released all the prisoners to join the battle.

On September 16th, on the anniversary of Mexican independence, the Stars and Stripes waved over the National Palace of Mexico City. Meanwhile, in the United States, many in Washington asked for the complete annexation of Mexico. The White House recalled Nicholas Trist, President Polk's envoy to negotiate peace, to receive new instructions and ask for more land, including the Lower California Peninsula, the Yucatan Peninsula, and the Isthmus of Tehuantepec, the thin strip of land where the Pacific and the Gulf of Mexico are closest. Trist was in a dilemma because he had already made progress in his negotiations and refused to return to Washington. Years later, Trist would confess to his family the shame that had overwhelmed him "during all the conferences, in the face of the unjust war." With the signing of the Treaty of Guadalupe-Hidalgo in February 1848, the territory of Mexico was reduced by half. After the partition, many Mexicans were left behind in the former provinces of what would become California, New Mexico, and Texas. Despite suffering abuse for many years, they managed to survive with their culture and traditions in a hostile environment. Their descendants were called "Chicanos"—a derivation of the Nahuatl word "Meshico"—and they still live in the southern United States, where they have become an increasingly relevant cultural, political, and economic presence.

Chapter 5 – The Big Division

Before losing half of its territory, Mexicans did not have much of a common identity. If the trauma of war and mutilation had any positive consequences, it was that people from different regions, from Baja California to Yucatan, began to realize that they shared a common history and destiny. Santa Anna, to whom practically the first period of independent Mexico belonged—to such an extent that those decades are known as "Santa Anna's Mexico"—became president once again in 1853, twenty years after his first inauguration. "Everything expects a remedy from General Santa Anna. Come then, as it has been announced, to your mission of saving Mexico from its ruins," published a newspaper of the time.

Despite suffering from territorial indigestion that would eventually lead to its own civil war, the United States continued to press Mexico for more land. Many voices in the north called for a complete annexation. In the next decade, the United States opened new claims on the border, given that its planned transcontinental train to the Pacific had to pass necessarily through Mexican soil since the American side was very mountainous. James Gadsden, the ambassador to Mexico, met with Santa Anna and showed him a map with the border that his country desired; it included not only the relatively small portion of land where the train should pass, but it also had an international line that was much farther south. In view of the occasion, Gadsden had fixed the line so that the peninsula of Baja California and the Mexican states of Sonora, Sinaloa, Durango, and Chihuahua would pass into the domain of the United States. If Mexico were to agree to this demand, its territory would once again be cut in half. A band of adventurers had just failed in their attempt to annex Baja California and Sonora to the United States, and it was as if the Texas situation was happening all over again. Santa Anna realized that the US was willing to go to a new war and would gladly seize another half from his country if he did not resolve the Mesilla issue soon. That was the name of the territory that the projected train would cut through, located in the modern states of Arizona and New Mexico.

The operation known as the "Gadsden Purchase" was signed in 1853; the Mexican government got 15 million dollars for 76,000 square kilometers. Thus, General Santa Anna acted with a practical sense and avoided war, but the people did not forgive him. Santa Anna, who was formerly a Liberal, became a kind of frivolous king who called himself "His Most Serene Highness"—just like Father Hidalgo in the Mexican War of Independence—and, to sustain the excesses of his extravagant court, he invented absurd taxes for the population, such as taxes on the number of windows in a house and taxes per pet, among others.

His last stay in the National Palace, however, left behind one of Mexico's distinctive marks. In 1853, Santa Anna organized a contest to choose a national anthem that would unite the Mexicans scattered across the north, south, and east. First, a contest was opened to choose the lyrics. There was a young and talented poet named Francisco González Bocanegra who did not dare to compete because he mostly wrote love poems. Bocanegra considered that a patriotic hymn was beyond his lyrical reach. As he resisted to enter the competition, despite his friends encouraging him to write, his girlfriend, disgusted, set him a small trap. With tricks, she walked him to an out-of-the-way room in her parents' house, pushed him inside, and immediately threw a padlock on the door, warning him that she wouldn't let him out until he wrote something. Four hours later, Francisco slipped under the door what would be the Mexican National Anthem. He won the contest by a unanimous vote.

Then the prize for the music was opened, which was appropriately won by a Spanish composer named Jaime Nunó, a director of several military bands. In this way, the two nations that had given birth to modern Mexico were founded in an anthem.

The verses of the hymn reflect the history and character of the country. With an almost apocalyptic tone, the poem is full of tragedy, rumors of war, waves of blood, strange enemies desecrating the homeland, towers and palaces crumbling down with horrid rumble, a mention of a grave, and God's implacable finger. The room in which Bocanegra was locked up held several scenes of the history of Mexico decorated on the walls, which inspired the poet to write the stanzas. The paintings must have been terrible. "O, Fatherland, ere your children, defenseless, bend their neck beneath the yoke, may your fields be watered with blood, may their foot be printed in blood. And may your temples, palaces and towers collapse with horrid clamor, and may their ruins continue on, saying: Of one thousand heroes, here the Fatherland once was."

The hymn was first performed officially on September 16th, 1854, Independence Day. The orchestra was conducted by director Jaime Nunó himself in the presence of an aged Santa Anna.

The Reform War

When a new uprising in the south overthrew Santa Anna, the eternal division between Liberals and Conservatives opened again, this time with more brutality. Liberals wanted a republic in the American style, one that was representative, federal, and popular, with separation between church and state. Above all, they wanted to expropriate the Catholic Church's property, which had great resources ever since the time of New Spain. The Church sometimes lent money to the government, and it possessed extensive assets, which, in many cases, were unproductive. The Conservatives, seeing the chaos in which the country had been in for several years, with its rebellious states and an inept and obstructive Congress that never accomplished anything, sought a strong, centralist state that was supported in the Church and the army.

The division had deep historical roots. The military disaster that ended in a defeat inflicted by the Americans sank the country in a period of dejection that permeated all aspects of social life. This situation gave rise to a self-critical examination of the national predicament and led to a renewed search for viable solutions to the problems that afflicted the country. The most eminent Conservatives proposed a change in the directions of politics, postulating the return to the old ways, and the preservation of institutions and modes of coexistence inherited from their Spanish past. Around these ideas, a conservative, oppositional, and militant party emerged with overwhelming force. The Conservatives aimed their ideological attacks to refute the Liberal doctrine, arguing that they wanted to save the country from the anarchy and ruin that, in their view, was imminent. They attributed this situation to the fact that independent Mexico had broken with its historical past to adopt government systems based on principles and institutions copied from foreign models; they postulated that Mexicans should strive to direct their efforts toward the country's reconstruction and that they should be inspired by feelings of respect for authority, religion, and property. Ultimately, after seeing uprising after uprising, as well as the gradual loss of territory, they came to propose a monarchy as the only way of salvation.

After Santa Anna's final fall, the so-called War of Reform erupted with unusual force. The country was divided between those who supported the new constitution of 1857, which decreed the freedom of religion, freedom of the press, and equality before the law, among other things, and those who opposed it. The situation was much more than political. The moment divided even families, where respect for the ecclesiastical authorities weighed against those who, like many sincere believers, considered that the Church should submit to political authority. The Reform War was not just another uprising of a rebel general to put one president in place of another. It was a revolution to define the country's direction. In the war, which was not regional but national, both sides committed unjust acts against the Church and civilians, demanding forced loans that would never be paid. Although they were defeated at the beginning, the Liberals managed to change the course of the war at the Battle of Silao in 1860. Conservatives dispersed into guerrilla factions as they continued to study how to secure the intervention of a European power.

In 1859, the Liberal president Benito Juárez had decreed the nationalization of clergy assets to pay debts to anxious foreign lenders and strengthen his government, which further aggravated the division. During the Reform War, there were two presidents, one in Veracruz and one in Mexico City, and both sides sought foreign help. Juárez offered more territory to the United States, but luckily for Mexico, the offer was rejected by the US Congress. In early 1861, Benito Juárez, who represented the new direction of the country, made his entrance into Mexico City and expelled members of the clergy, including bishops and ambassadors from countries that had not supported him. But the hostilities were far from over. From the outset, the government was still bankrupt. The value of the Church's properties had been overestimated, many assets had been wasted, and the ministers were not able to organize public finances. Much to his dismay, Juárez, with progressive ideas but an empty national treasury, was forced to suspend the payment of the external debt. The dice were cast, and Mexico's next chapter is one of the most dramatic and studied moments of its existence, despite having been brief: a monarchy. And it was just not any monarchy—it was an empire.

Chapter 6 – "The Most Beautiful Empire in the World"

"Our enemies may be the best soldiers in the world,

but you are the best children of Mexico."

Ignacio Zaragoza to his men, Battle of Puebla, Cinco de Mayo

In those days, declaring a suspension of external debt payments was no small feat, especially when the debtors were Britain, France, and Spain. France was under Napoleon III, who had promised to extend his dominion overseas, and Spain, although it had diplomatic relations with Mexico, was still distrustful toward its former colony, and it had even contemplated reconquest. As soon as President Juárez announced that he could not pay, the three nations sent their war fleets to Mexico to collectively demand, at gunpoint, the interest payments. When they arrived in Veracruz, where Hernán Cortés and Winfield Scott had landed on their way to the capital, the tripartite alliance seized the customs of the most important ports in the Gulf. The representative of Mexico met with the commission and guaranteed the Europeans that the country could and would pay.

However, one of the three countries had further intentions besides the purely financial. Napoleon III had bought into the idea that he could establish a monarchy in Mexico and have an ally that would help him curb the expansion of the United States and protect the culture of Latin America—a term coined by him—from the Anglo-Saxon Protestant advance. Napoleon also had hopes on a projected canal in Nicaragua or one crossing the Isthmus of Tehuantepec. When Spain and Britain realized that the troops of Napoleon III did not plan to retire but instead march to Mexico City and take the country, they washed their hands and sailed back to Europe. An alarmed Juárez saw how a new formidable threat loomed over Mexico, while the French minister Dubois de Saligny published a manifesto to the Mexicans, where he reiterated that France harbored no bad intentions.

Mexicans, we did not come to take sides in your divisions. We have come to put an end to them. What we want is to invite all men of good will to join the consolidation of order, the regeneration of this great country. And to give proof of our sincere desire for conciliation...we have asked you to accept our help to establish a state of affairs in Mexico that prevents us from having to organize these expensive expeditions again.

When the army of the *Pantalons Rouge*, under the command of Charles de Lorencez, saw the city of Puebla in the distance, they were practically at the gates of the capital. General Lorencez wrote to Napoleon III that he had such military and human superiority over the Mexicans that he could already be considered Mexico's master. French minister Saligny assured Lorencez that the Mexicans would greet him with a shower of flowers in Puebla.

The Battle of Cinco de Mayo

Juárez was ready for the possibility of a government in exile, but first, he sent his best general to try to stop the French. Ignacio Zaragoza was born in Texas when it was still a Mexican province, and he looked more like a seminary student than a soldier. At the gates of Puebla, some recommended Lorencez to pass by and go directly to Mexico City, but there was still the Guadalupe fort on a hill to deal with, as Zaragoza's forces were waiting there, many of them peasants with moth-eaten weapons. Lorencez decided to take the city, certain that any resistance would crumble in half an hour. In the war against the United States fifteen years earlier, the Mexican Army used to withdraw amid chaos, running in panic and looting everything in its pass after a collapse. Zaragoza was careful to impose order and discipline. Many civilian volunteers showed up in the Mexican countryside to help dig trenches and lift barriers. Some asked to join the defense army, but they had to be taught how to even load a rifle.

Lorencez's plan was simple: pulverize the fortification with cannon blasts and then liquidate the survivors with the cavalry. The bell of Puebla's cathedral rang at ten o'clock in the morning when the French moved in, and the terrified citizens locked themselves in their houses. The streets became deserted. When Lorencez thought that he had broken the defense line, he charged with a column that met a shower of gunshots from the Mexicans, who not only stood firm but also threw themselves against the French. At the top of Guadalupe Hill, there ensued bloody hand-to-hand combat between Mexicans and the fierce Zouaves, a French light infantry regiment fresh from the Foreign Legion. At four o'clock in the afternoon, the French, baffled, were in retreat, and Zaragoza's cavalry went after them. When the world's most powerful army was defeated, the Mexican general telegraphed the president, "The national arms have been covered with glory." It read like something out of the national anthem. The date was May 5th, 1862.

The news was received in France with stupor. Although Napoleon would return almost a year later with a force five times greater—25,000 elite soldiers—the delay of one year in Napoleon's plans proved critical for the eventual collapse of the Mexican monarchy. Almost oblivious to this drama, at Miramar Castle in Italy, Austrian Archduke Maximilian of Habsburg was receiving a Mexican commission that offered him the crown of Mexico. "We are lost if Europe does not come to our aid," wrote one of the most intelligent

Conservatives, Lucas Alamán, and the Mexicans who went to Maximilian and his wife, Princess Charlotte of Belgium, were doing just that. They asked the couple to be the monarchs of the old Montezuma empire. They were not traitors, as later history would portray them. They actually had the sincere conviction that only a strong monarchy sponsored by a world power could save Mexico from disintegration.

The Crown of Mexico

Maximilian of Habsburg, the brother of Emperor Franz Joseph I of the Austro-Hungarian Empire, was a man of liberal ideas. He was polite, idealistic, and skeptical that Mexicans really wanted him in the country. He first demanded evidence that he would not be an imposition, and when he was presented with an alleged plebiscite with the signatures of 75 percent of Mexicans, he accepted the throne and promised that "he would establish *liberal* wise institutions and order." The Mexican commission, which was made of Conservatives, winced at those words, but it was too late to turn back. Maximilian was never completely convinced of the adventure, as it was full of risks and far from his beloved Castle of Miramar, where he liked to take care of his botanical garden, sail, and make exploratory trips around the world, but his wife Charlotte, one of the most beautiful and educated princesses in Europe, talked him into it. The most they had achieved so far was the viceroyalty of the tiny territory of Lombardy-Venice. Mexico, by comparison, was three times more extensive than the powerful Austro-Hungarian Empire of Maximilian's brother, Franz Joseph.

Charlotte, barely 23 years old, had been educated to be the head of state. She spoke French, German, Flemish, and English, and she knew about diplomacy, international politics, and even military science. What she most feared at the time, as she wrote in 1866, was to stay "to contemplate a rock until the age of sixty," referring to the cliff where the couple's castle was built. In April 1864, Maximiliano and Carlota, their adopted names for Spanish-speaking Mexico, boarded the ship to America. They stopped in Rome to receive the blessing of Pope Pius IX, heard mass in the Vatican, and then entered the Atlantic. Less than a month later, from the deck of the *Novara*, they saw the Pico de Orizaba, the highest mountain in Mexico, visible from 200 kilometers (a little over 124 miles) away. When Maximiliano touched the port of Veracruz at nine in the morning, he read a proclamation before the people who were there to welcome him. "Mexicans, you have desired me." He descended the steps and stepped on Mexican soil. It was, however, in Orizaba, 130 kilometers (almost 81 miles) inland where they were given their first formal reception and experienced real contact, which bordered on adoration, from the people. Before entering the city, the Native Americans approached the cortege, disengaged the mules from the carriage, and stood in front of it to pull it themselves along the main avenue. Maximilian flushed with embarrassment. He vehemently refused to let the Native Americans transport him as if they were beasts of burden, but they insisted so much, and the newcomers were so determined to not allow such treatment, that they had to descend and walk to Orizaba, with its streets replete with flower arcs.

Halfway to the capital, the couple made another stop in Puebla, the site of the famous battle of Cinco de Mayo, where the reception was warm. Many Mexicans, despite everything, were willing to grant them the benefit of the doubt. They had some hope that perhaps that well-intentioned rulers could stop the constant revolutions, forced recruitment, and disintegration of territory. Above all, they wanted someone to help the forgotten ones, those who had been watching all their lives as one general after another fought for the presidency: the Native Americans, the original owners of the land, who were still the majority of the country's population.

Many people in Puebla welcomed them from the balconies. Several men on horseback, along with their children, escorted them downtown. The bells rang, and the couple received a new shot of confidence. While they were in the city, Carlota (Charlotte) turned

24, and the people greeted her, but after seeing the unfortunate state of hospitals, orphanages, and schools, she corroborated what she had suspected since her arrival: that the country was destroyed after six decades of civil war. Stunned by the social disparity, Princess Carlota wrote that Mexico presented unforgivable contrasts. "If a country was ever miraculously saved from a state from which it could not emerge, I am sure it will be now." The reception in Mexico was even more enthusiastic. The historic center of Mexico City was crowded with the parade of the *Pantalons Rouge*, Napoleon's soldiers, while the new monarchs passed under flower arcs. Juárez and his government had gone into exile.

The couple was crowned in the cathedral of Mexico City on April 10th, 1864. They stayed the night in the National Palace, but the building was in a deplorable state. The first night, Maximilian had to sleep on a pool table because there were bed bugs. Soon, they found the place they were looking for. About eight kilometers (almost five miles) from the city was Chapultepec Castle, which had been built by Bernardo Gálvez on a rocky hill, although during the time of Maximilian, it was in ruins. Maximiliano, a natural optimist, set out to adapt it for his court. In a short amount of time, the old refurbished castle became the seat of the imperial government.

A Liberal Empire

In spite of many acts that the Liberals mockingly called ridiculous excesses of Maximiliano and Carlota—such as having a whole ceremony for their court and their lavish receptions at Chapultepec Castle—the monarchs were not despots nor did they lack sensitivity toward the population. Their first act was to receive a delegation of Native Americans who brought complaints about their ancestral lands. The monarchs went even further and tried to establish politics that nobody had ever dreamed of in Mexico: abolition of work for minors, freedom of worship, freedom of the press, limited workdays with two days off, the prohibition of corporal punishment, freedom to choose where to work, the obligation of employers to pay in cash (an absolute novelty), compulsory and free school for all children, the attraction of foreign scientists and technicians, the establishment of a drainage system in the cities, the planting of trees and the obligation of citizens to care for them, land property rights for peasants, freedom from peonage, and improvement of hospitals, nursing homes, and charitable houses. These measures sought to establish the basis for a liberal but human economic system, a kind of proto-social democracy.

Much less known were their plans, which were never openly expressed, to recover Central America and the Caribbean or to at least extend Mexico's sphere of influence to the south and east, establishing Yucatan as the gravitation center from which Mexico would become a continental power. But things were not going to work out for them. For a while, the empire achieved sufficient stability to be recognized by European nations, but in 1866, things started to change.

The Conservatives that had brought Maximilian were disappointed with him, as he was even more progressive than the hated Juárez. The Church and the Vatican withdrew their support because the emperor did not reverse the reform laws or restore the Church its property. And the Liberals, who supported Juárez in exile, called Maximiliano and Carlota tyrants. No one was happy with the young rulers. Even more decisive was the entry of the United States to the stage. The US had never approved European interference in the continent. Presidents Abraham Lincoln and Juárez had supported each other, and the Americans considered it inadmissible to have a monarchy sponsored by France on the other side of the Rio Grande. The US Civil War had prevented the country from intervening in Mexico and helping the Liberals. In 1866, though, things were different. Finally, Napoleon III became so overwhelmed with problems back in Paris, with the emergence of Otto von Bismarck's unified Germany, and Napoleon complained that his best generals were in Mexico. When Napoleon III announced that he was going to withdraw his troops in America, Maximilian understood that the days of his empire were numbered.

In 1866, President Andrew Johnson helped supply Juárez and his followers with weapons and American combatants eager to do something after the end of the Civil War. Juárez's men with their foreign reinforcements and began to move south, reconquering territories, while France withdrew from Mexico. Napoleon III did not want to risk going to war with the United States. At the end of June 1866, he announced the gradual removal of his troops and advised Maximilian to abdicate. Maximilian considered the possibility of going back to Austria, but Princess Charlotte was stubbornly opposed. Desperate, seeing how they were losing more and more territory, she offered to go to Europe herself to appeal before Napoleon.

The Liberals heard of Carlota's departure to Europe, and they took it as a sign that the empire was crumbling and gained momentum. When Mexico City was being surrounded, Maximiliano's advisors urged him to leave the capital and gather his forces in Querétaro, a city that had been fortified years before by French General François Bazaine. After more than two months of hunger, siege, and gunfire, the besieged were eating horse and mule meat. Maximilian's men melted the church bells, the pipes, and all the pieces of metal they found to make ammunition. The last French soldiers left the country, and the emperor was left with a few faithful men of his Austrian guard and the remnants of the Conservative army, which was led by Miguel Miramón and Tomás Mejía. In the end, one of Maximiliano's men decided to hand over the city and let the enemy in. The emperor was arrested. After a trial, which was lost beforehand, he was sentenced to be shot on Cerro de las Campanas, located on the outskirts of the city of Querétaro.

Juárez was back in power. Although several international personalities—among them the writer Victor Hugo of *Les Misérables* fame— pleaded for Maximillian's life, Maximillian was still taken to

Cerro de las Campanas on June 19th, 1867. When the emperor saw the hill, he exclaimed, "That's where I planned to unfurl the victory flag, and that's where I'm going to die. Life is a comedy!" He shook hands with each one of the soldiers who were going to shoot him. Some grieving, he comforted them by telling them that they were soldiers and should do their duty. He also handed each one a gold coin and asked them not to shoot his face so that his mother could recognize him. "I will die for a just cause" were his last words. "I forgive everyone and I also beg everyone to forgive me. May my blood seal the misfortunes of this country. Long live Mexico. *Viva Mexico!*" A few seconds later, the Austrian archduke, who had so desired for Mexico to prosper, lay dead.

And Carlota? The empress had arrived in Paris to an aging Napoleon III, begging him not to withdraw his support for Mexico. Then she went to the Vatican to kneel before the pope, trying to fix things with the Church. But at the see of San Pedro, the princess lost the battle. Her mind collapsed. Charlotte began to speak in all the languages she knew, intermingled, trembling violently, saying that Napoleon had sent assassins to kill her. Unable to hold back the tears, she begged a stunned Pope Pius IX to protect her. She immediately wrote her last letter to Maximilian, sure she had been poisoned and was going to die. But the princess did not die. Seeing that she had gone mad, her family locked her up in a castle in Belgium, where she lived for sixty more years in the darkness of insanity. In Mexico, she is still remembered with a ditty from that time: "Goodbye, Mama Carlota, goodbye, my tender love."

Chapter 7 – In the Times of Don Porfirio

"There was a Strong Man of the Americas. A dazzling future was prophesied, a golden era had arrived already, and the stock phrase was that Mexico had abandoned her turbulent, unproductive past and begun to take her rightful place among the sisterhood of nations."

—Anita Brenner

A triumphant Benito Juárez entered Mexico City on July 21ˢᵗ, 1867, accompanied by his most prominent general, Porfirio Díaz, who had recovered the capital a month earlier. This period is known as the restoration of the republic. It was the definitive triumph of the Liberals, and Juárez became the greatest hero of the republic in textbooks. Mexico City's international airport, a large city in the north of the country, and countless schools and avenues today bear his name. But in the last years of his life, when he was almost in his seventies, he clung to the presidency and provoked new uprisings in different parts of the country. Since the fall of the empire, the presidents had moved to Chapultepec Castle. Juárez considered it an excessive luxury and established his home in modest rooms in the National Palace. It was there that he died of heart disease. In his last hours, they spilled boiling water on his infarcted chest to revive him, to no avail.

The restoration of the republic did not change the country's maladies, as it suffered one uprising after another. Tired of this situation, the young general Porfirio Díaz rebelled under the Plan of Tuxtepec, which was "a revolution to end all revolutions." Díaz had been famous since the Battle of Puebla on May 5th, 1862, where he had shown fearless and heroic behavior. Under his Plan of Tuxtepec, Díaz defeated the government forces, appointed an interim president, and a year later, in 1877, he became president through a legal election, which was helped by his belief in no more reelections. Ironies of life, he would become the longest-standing president in Mexico's history: he was reelected several times for a total of 33 years, effectively governing Mexico from the 19th to the early 20th century.

Porfirio Díaz Mori, who took a poor country into his hands and delivered a more advanced nation, is a controversial character. On the one hand, he achieved what the country had longed for so long and since its birth had been unable to achieve: political stability. In the first half-century of independent Mexico, only one president had completed his term peacefully. One of them, Santa Anna, had been president eleven times, at his own whim. Two presidents lasted two months in office, others lasted less than a week, and one of them only a day. Díaz stayed at the National Palace for 33 years thanks to a hard-handed policy, the rapid elimination of his opponents, and muzzling the press. Díaz achieved the long-awaited integration of the country, which was a formerly disjointed group of isolated regions. When Porfirio Díaz came to power, there was only one railroad from Veracruz to Mexico (the Cortés route), 640 kilometers (almost 398 miles) long. Transport and commerce to the rest of the country were carried on the backs of mules. At the end of this period, almost 20,000 kilometers (a little over 12,425 miles) of railroad tracks zigzagged throughout the republic. The population increased thanks to the end of the wars and advances in public health, and it passed from nine to fifteen million, the largest population since the end of the Spanish-Aztec war. With the new infrastructure in place, people of central Mexico began to migrate and populate other areas, especially the northern states.

In its first industrial revolution, foreign investments flowed to the mining industry, railroads, ports, and lucrative crops such as coffee. Díaz and his ministers were sagacious enough to clean up the country's foreign relations and ride the so-called first great wave of globalization, which occurred in the last quarter of the 19th century. For the first time in its history, Mexico became an exporting nation. No foreign power threatened the country during the Díaz dictatorship. On the contrary, Mexico established optimum commercial and diplomatic relations with the United States, Britain, Spain, and even France, whose armies Díaz had fought in Puebla on May 5th all those years ago. Porfirio Díaz was the first to meet with a president of the United States, William Taft, in El Paso-Ciudad Juárez. "You are, to my knowledge," said the old general to his neighbor, "the first US premier to visit this land."

It was an era of reconstruction, pacification, and unification but also of repression. Díaz's first objective was to pacify the country, and to achieve this, he did not hesitate to eliminate, exile, and bribe the military and many intellectuals. He also made changes in Congress to eliminate the opposition. He reconciled with the Catholic Church and the old Conservatives to keep the peace. A very weakened Church received a vital push with Díaz, who allowed it to own property again. The clergy opened up charitable congregations and confessional schools, while Díaz attended the coronation of the Virgin of Guadalupe in 1892. Through all of this, without having to abrogate Juárez's laws, the president had the clergy on his side. Consequently, the Church stopped supporting, as it had done in the past, rebellions that were launched for the alleged defense of religion. With the Porfirian peace, the arts flourished with important people such as the poets Amado Nervo and Manuel Gutiérrez Nájera, the artists José Guadalupe Posada and Saturnino Herrán, the composer Juventino Rosas, and the novelist Ignacio Manuel Altamirano. Díaz seemed to have achieved what his predecessors had missed: a healthy balance between the Conservatives and the Liberals.

But not everything was rosy. Notwithstanding all the new infrastructure, most of the railroads, ports, mines, and haciendas were controlled by foreign investors who had gotten very generous concessions. The United States, in particular, seemed to be taking over Mexico with abusive conditions. There was no need to swallow more territory with this new form of conquest. Díaz himself acknowledged the situation when he uttered a famous remark that Mexicans still repeat: "Poor Mexico! So far from God and so close to the United States." Agriculture flourished but only in export crops whose demand was increasing in the international markets, such as coffee, rubber, and henequen. Instead, the production of goods for the common people, which included corn, beans, wheat, and chili, decreased, and families began to starve. Inequality and the concentration of wealth increased. Large coffee, henequen, and rubber corporations absorbed communal lands and created a new caste of eternally indebted peasants.

One of the least remembered aspects of the Porfiriato, the name given to Porfirio Díaz's dictatorship, was the fierce repression of indigenous peoples, especially the Yaqui in Sonora and the Maya in Yucatan. It was around this time that a rebellion broke out in the Yucatan Peninsula, one different from all the previous indigenous wars. The life of the Mayas had not improved since the time of the Spanish conquest; indeed, it had only worsened.

The Caste War

The Mayas in Yucatan were a fiercely independent people that the Spanish had never been able to control. Since the colonial era, they had resisted white authority in many ways. In the second half of the 19th century, their situation was unbearable. The capitalist production of henequen, also known as sisal, on large haciendas only aggravated their situation. Henequen was a lucrative agave crop whose fibers were used to make ropes for boats, fabric, sacks, and other items that had a robust demand. American journalist John Kenneth Turner visited the haciendas in Yucatan at the time of Díaz and was horrified by what he saw. According to Turner, slavery persisted in Yucatan, if not officially called that in practice. "I didn't see worse punishments than beatings [on the Mayas] in Yucatan," he wrote. "Women are required to kneel to be beaten, as sometimes are men of great weight. Men and women are beaten in the fields as well as at the morning roll call. Each foreman, or capata, carries a heavy cane with which he punches and prods and whacks the slaves at will. I do not remember visiting a single field in which I did not see some of this punching and prodding and whacking going on."

The Mayas could not take it anymore and began the Caste War in 1847. It started out in a village near Mérida, where several Mayas, who were provided with food and weapons, gathered at the house of a leader named Jacinto Pat. The plan was to slaughter all the whites, proclaim the independence of the Maya, and crown a man called Cecilio Chi as their king. The authorities discovered the conspiracy, and after arresting and executing the rebels, they burned the town of Tepich, without letting women, the elderly, and children leave. The next day, Chi's men killed all the whites and mestizos, leaving only a few women behind in order to rape them, more out of hate than pleasure.

The Caste War became a war of mutual extermination, where the Mayas effectively sought to nullify the Spanish conquest, expel all the whites, and proclaim themselves autonomous and sovereign under their old laws and customs. What began as a local phenomenon became a racial war that spread throughout the Yucatan Peninsula and lasted more than half a century. When the rebels took a town or village, they slaughtered the population, and it was common for them to kill men with machetes, even when they had guns at hand. In retaliation, Mayan homes were burned by the government forces.

The white Yucatec, once again, went to the United States to seek help and protection, which they were not obtaining from Mexico. One of the principal men in Mérida, Justo Sierra O'Reilly, met with President James K. Polk in Washington, DC, and urged him to send help since the Mayas were in a war of extermination against the white population and very close to accomplishing it. The whites and mestizos in Yucatan, who were near the point of hysteria, were concentrated in the city of Mérida, which the Mayas were surrounding. Most families moved downtown to gain some protection inside the city walls. O'Reilly offered Yucatan's annexation to the United States in exchange for help, but luckily for Mexico, political intrigues and rivalries in the US prevented the factions from reaching an agreement. The governor also offered the peninsula to Spain.

When Mérida was surrounded, the governor tried to order an evacuation, but he couldn't find paper in his office to print the proclamation.

Rumors ran through the streets that savages were everywhere. People escaped to the sea from [the port of] Sisal, Campeche or any other port where they could grab anything that floated, to take them anywhere. In the streets of Mérida and Campeche there was talk of general slaughter, elimination of the white population of Yucatan, which meant more than 140 thousand people, counting the mestizos.

But when the apocalypse was imminent, the terrified whites saw a miracle happen: the Maya suddenly left the site. A cloud of insects had appeared, winged ants, which for the Mayas announced the beginning of rains, meaning it was time to return to their crops. Years later, the son of one of the leaders explained:

It was scorching heat. Suddenly there appeared the winged ants in great clouds from the north, south, east and west, all over the place. When they saw this, those with my father said to each other, and said to their brothers, "The time has come for us to do our plantation, because if we do not do it, we will not have the Grace of God to fill our children´s belly." Thus they said and argued, and thought a lot, and when the morning came, my father's men said each one: "I'm leaving." And despite the pleas and threats of the bosses, each man rolled up his blanket and prepared his food bag, tightened the straps of his sandals and set off toward his house and his cornfield. Then the Batabob, knowing that it was useless to attack the city with the few remaining men, met in council and decided to go back home.

Mérida was saved for the time being, but the rebellion did not end. The Mayas, who had adopted the name of *Cruzoob* or "Crusaders," retreated south into the jungles and proclaimed the independent republic of Santa Cruz, which was recognized by Great Britain. For a very short time, there was a true Mayan nation in the 19th century, located in the extreme south of Mexico (in the modern state of Quintana Roo), resisting the constant siege of the government. That was until a new and terrible weapon arrived, the multi-shot rifle or machine gun, which caused horror among the Maya. It was hard to avoid a single shot charging with their machetes, but to throw themselves at the new machine guns was suicide. The Mayan chiefs of the different regions met in the city of Chan Santa Cruz, and after checking the lack of gunpowder, ammunition, and corn, they decided to set fire to the town and disperse in small groups. They entered the jungle and promised to meet again every full moon. In this way, under the presidency of Porfirio Díaz, the long resistance of the Maya came to an end in 1901. And thus ended the last great indigenous rebellion on the American continent.

Chapter 8 – The Mexican Revolution

In 1910, Porfirio Díaz was eighty years old and a relic. He had been born when California and Texas were still a part of Mexico. He had fought in the famous battle of Cinco de Mayo to stop the French and the monarchy. Most people in the country did not remember any other president than Díaz. Mexico enjoyed the Porfirian peace that was already being compared by some skeptics to the peace of the graveyards. He had been reelected six times, and although to a foreign observer, there was no need for social change since business was flourishing in Mexico, there was clear economic, political, and social unrest throughout the nation. Ninety percent of the country's inhabitants lived in poverty, and more than three-quarters of the population was indigenous. According to the country's ruling class, they were a burden, an ignorant and lazy mass, who were meant to be oppressed, subjugated, and exploited to death under the sun. "We were tough," admitted Díaz at the end of his era. "The poor are so ignorant that they have no power. We were tough. Sometimes to the point of being cruel. But all this was necessary for the life and progress of the nation."

Mexico entered the 20th century amidst workers' agitation. In the last years of Díaz's long tenure, the laborers began to rebel and were harshly repressed. Don Porfirio, as he was and is still called, always resolved in favor of foreign interests; for him, it was vital to maintain peace and order and preserve the confidence of international investors. But in 1908, the old dictator gave an interview to a North American journalist named James Creelman, where he finally conceded that he had had enough and that he would welcome the emergence of an opposition party. "I will welcome an opposition party. If it appears, I will see it as a blessing and not as an evil, and if it can develop power, not to exploit but to rule, I will stand by it, support it, advise it and forget myself in the successful inauguration of complete democratic government in the country." The interview provoked a hornet's nest. A son of a landowner with democratic ideals named Francisco Ignacio Madero began to campaign against Díaz, organizing a political party and touring the country. When Díaz sent him to jail and had himself reelected for the seventh time in the 1910 election, Madero realized that an armed revolution was the only way to democracy. He issued the Plan of San Luis, which called on all Mexicans to rise up against the dictatorship on November 20th, 1910.

The Mexican Revolution

The Mexican Revolution, which ran from 1910 to 1920, began as a democratic movement to oust President Díaz but ended up as a socialist revolution. At the same time, on the other side of the world, Vladimir Lenin called on the Russians to create a utopia controlled by the workers. Madero's call to arms did not generate much response among the middle, urban, and intellectual classes. But another sector, possibly the most exhausted, responded at first with some hesitation but then with unusual energy: the peasant class of northern and southern Mexico.

The world watched the Mexican Revolution with interest, and the movement grew uncontrollable. Two characters embody this important period better than anyone else. In the north, one of the most essential figures of the country's history appeared, Francisco "Pancho" Villa, who is known through many photographs as the archetype of the Mexican man: tall and stocky, wide hat, mustache, horse, gun in his hand, and a bullet-crossed chest. This northerner was driven by more than the democratic cause. He fought like a possessed man, holding hatred for the regime and against everything that reminded him of dictator Díaz, including the landowners and the rural guards who had harassed him for years. In one battle, Villa tricked the army by planting sticks with hats so that it would appear he had a larger force, which helped to instill panic among the enemy ranks. Besides his military genius, Villa had charisma: he gathered soldiers and volunteers from nothing, and people saw in him a symbol of their rage against a government that had forgotten the peasants. As such, legends began to be woven around him. He took Ciudad Juárez, a strategic point on the border with the United States, after two days of battle. US neighbors watched the clash from the other side, lying on the roof of train wagons to avoid loose bullets.

The other figure, almost a mirror of Villa, emerged at the other end of Mexico, in the southern mountains. He was tall, dark, and good-looking, with an even wider hat and a slightly old-fashioned mustache. Emiliano Zapata, a peasant leader, began to take the lands of the haciendas by force and distributed it among the people of Anenecuilco, his hometown. Zapata strengthened his legitimacy by rejecting bribes and the temptation of self-benefit. He once said, "Check the Colonial titles and take what is owed to the people." In a few months, he managed to gather an army of twelve thousand peasants. He entered Cuautla, his first major city, while his peasants carried banners of the Virgin of Guadalupe.

Both unique cases in Mexico's history, for so long a country of military men conspiring to seize power, neither Villa nor Zapata were interested in the presidency or any other political position, although they had the possibility of sitting on the chair. Pancho Villa openly acknowledged that he was an uneducated man and only wanted justice for the humble. Zapata said that the chair had the power to change people. "I'd rather not sit down," he said when he had it in front of him in the National Palace, "because when someone is good, and sits on this chair, when he gets up he's become bad." Madero won the election in what was perhaps the first democratic exercise in the history of Mexico, winning 99 percent of the popular vote, but he did not last long. As he was an idealist who could not control the magnitude of the forces he had unleashed, in 1913, he was in conflict with everyone—he could not decide to resolve once and for all the peasants' demands. Worst of all, he was surrounded by adversaries, with a vociferous press that took advantage of the same freedom he had given them. In February, he was killed in a tangled conspiracy, which the US ambassador had a lot to do with, that had been orchestrated by an old general named Victoriano Huerta. After appointing an interim president, who lasted in power a ridiculous 45 minutes—a record in history—General Huerta became Mexico's new dictator. His act enraged all the factions—Villa, Zapata, and the others—who united around a common goal: to overthrow the traitor who, with a bullet, had destroyed Mexico's opportunity to become a democratic country.

At the end of 1914, the powerful armies of Pancho Villa from the north—the famous "Dorados," which was followed by thousands of women to cook for them—and Emiliano Zapata from the south—mostly Native American peasants with white cotton pants—marched into Mexico City a few days apart. In December, the two popular leaders were photographed together in the National Palace around the presidential chair. Villa sat on it, laughing. It was a unique moment that has never been repeated. They themselves did not understand the true magnitude of what was happening. For the first time in Mexico's history, two popular armies had captured power. However, neither Villa nor Zapata knew what to do with it. They could have ordered anything, but neither of them had the intellectual capacity or desire to be president, and they were the first to admit it.

They put a puppet president in the National Palace and let the historical opportunity pass. Soon, others would seize the void they had left. The Mexican Revolution was fragmented into many leaders fighting against one another. Zapata returned to his southern mountains, and Villa lost a disastrous battle in Celaya. His powerful northern division never recovered from the blow and fragmented. At the end of 1916, Pancho Villa was isolated in the north with just a few faithful men, being hunted as a vulgar bandit, when he decided to attack the United States.

It was not a large-scale invasion. Villa was with no more than four hundred men, but it is the only time to date that the continental United States has been invaded by an army with their boots on the ground. Around four o'clock in the morning, Villa burst into the town of Columbus, New Mexico, as the people slept peacefully. The Villistas attacked from four directions, aiming everywhere, looting, and unleashing chaos. The inhabitants woke up terrified. From afar, people could see the glow of farms and houses engulfed in flames, and they could hear the wild cries of the Villistas, who had seized about one hundred horses as well as ammunition.

In the United States, many outraged and opportunistic voices called for a new intervention to punish Mexico, but with World War I going on in Europe, President Woodrow Wilson knew that the path of prudence was best. However, he still sent an expedition under the command of General John J. Pershing and ten thousand men to capture Villa. "Where is Pancho Villa?" Pershing asked in his broken Spanish in each ranch and village in the mountains. "He went that way, to the next town uphill," the women answered, covering half their faces with a rebozo. When the next hamlet appeared, the men on horseback loaded their rifles and blocked the escape routes. "Is Pancho Villa here?" Pershing roared. "Villa has just left, *señor*. If you go that way, you will surely reach him in half an hour," the locals responded, pointing toward the opposite side. "I have the honor of informing you," Pershing wrote his report at the end of the day, "that Francisco Villa is everywhere and nowhere." The punitive expedition returned to the United States without fulfilling its objective.

In private, the famous military general later admitted that "when the true history is written, it will not be a very inspiring chapter for school children, or even grownups to contemplate. Having dashed into Mexico with the intention of eating the Mexicans raw, we turned back at the first repulse and are now sneaking home under cover, like a whipped cur with its tail between its legs."

The Zimmermann Telegram

During the Mexican Revolution, Mexico became involved in an incident that changed the course of world history. In 1917, in the middle of World War I, Germany launched an ambitious plan. The United States took notice when the British intelligence service intercepted a telegram sent by German Foreign Secretary Arthur Zimmermann to the German ambassador in Mexico, Heinrich von Eckardt. When the British showed the paper to the US embassy in London, the Americans thought it was a joke. But once they learned it was authentic, and its content was disseminated in the American press, the American people burned with indignation. In the telegram, Arthur Zimmermann instructed the ambassador to begin negotiations with the president of Mexico, Venustiano Carranza, so that, with German support, Mexico could declare war on the US. In return, it would get "generous financial support," and if the Central Powers won World War I, Mexico would recover the states of Texas, New Mexico, and Arizona, the territories that were lost in 1847. The telegram, decoded by the intelligence of Great Britain, said:

We intend to begin on the first of February unrestricted submarine warfare. We shall endeavor in spite of this to keep the United States of America neutral. In the event of this not succeeding, we make Mexico a proposal of alliance on the following basis: make war together, make peace together, generous financial support and an understanding on our part that Mexico is to reconquer the lost territory in Texas, New Mexico, and Arizona. The settlement in detail is left to you. You will inform the President of the above most secretly as soon as the outbreak of war with the United States of America is certain, and add the suggestion that he should, on his own initiative, invite Japan to immediate adherence and at the same time mediate between Japan and ourselves. Please call the President's attention to the fact that the ruthless employment of our submarines now offers the prospect of compelling England in a few months to make peace. Signed, ZIMMERMANN.

Although the telegram did not actually reach Carranza, the Mexican president sent his foreign minister to talk with Heinrich von Eckardt, who had been sent from Berlin. Carranza also established a commission to investigate whether Mexico should agree to the terms of the telegram. The Germans promised money and weapons to help wage war on the United States, but most likely, Carranza was not taking the Germans seriously, and he was just trying to get funds from whatever source in order to consolidate his power with minimal commitment. On April 14th, 1917, Carranza formally declined Zimmermann's proposal, but he did not close all the doors. "If Mexico is dragged into the [First] World War in spite of everything, we'll see. For now the alliance has been frustrated, but it will be necessary later on at a certain moment." The Zimmermann Telegram threw the hitherto neutral United States into the First World War. The telegram's plan went nowhere, but its content again aroused suspicions against the southern neighbor of the US, and the remembrance of the territories lost in 1847 once more removed consciences on both sides of the border.

In 1919, Carranza was firmly in power. The United States had recognized his government, and his main enemies had vanished. Villa remained hidden in the northern mountains, protected by the local population. After a decade and a million deaths (7 percent of the population but a much higher percentage of the economically active population), the Mexican Revolution, which was initially started to restore democracy and then to regenerate the country's economic system, proved to be the most expensive war, in terms of both money and human lives, in Mexico's history. But the long struggle did raise awareness of the need for social justice, starting with land distribution and education for the common people. The ideals promoted by fighters such as Madero, Villa, and especially Zapata were embodied in a new constitution promulgated in 1917, which still governs the land today.

The Mexican Revolution of 1910, a decisive event in the formation of 20th-century Mexico's philosophy, economy, and even artistic development, brought the rise of middle and popular classes and the displacement of the oligarchy that had run the show throughout almost all of the 19th century. In its first stage, the revolution was initiated by just another elite, but the popular classes took it from their hands. From 1913 on, the middle class assumed the leadership, and the peasant classes were positioned for the first time as a formidable political force with a voice and vote in the country's development. The new state, born in 1920 when the bullets stopped flying and the dust settled, was not democratic, but it was indeed nationalist and popular. It spawned authoritarian leaders, but they were men forged in the Mexican Revolution, and so, they had a social conscience and willingness to carry out a comprehensive agrarian reform and the organization of the working class. Finally, a stable state was born, with great popular support and with the reluctant acceptance of the United States.

It was the surviving revolutionaries and the followers of those who had begun the great social departure—Zapata, Madero, Carranza, and Villa, who were all killed by their enemies—who created the new Mexican identity. After a hundred years of calamities, the country seemed to have found a route that could accommodate everyone. The revolutionaries integrated the whole country into a new nationalist state that was not xenophobic; it was revolutionary but with stable institutions.

It fell on the great Mexican artists from the 1920s onward—painters Diego Rivera, Frida Kahlo, and José Clemente Orozco; writers Juan Rulfo and Octavio Paz; musicians Manuel M. Ponce, Carlos Chávez, and José Pablo Moncayo—to show what Mexicanity means. Thanks to them, and others of their generation, Mexico began to be recognized as a country full of people with cultural expressions on par with the rest of the world.

Chapter 9 – The Cristeros

"The Church has exceeded our wildest hopes in decreeing the suspension of religious services; nothing could be more pleasing to us. We have got the clergy by the throat and will do everything to strangle it."

—Mexican Minister of Interior, Adalberto Tejeda, 1926

The Mexican Revolution produced the Constitution of 1917 and a political class that abhorred the Catholic Church, which was, nonetheless, still the predominant religion of the country. During the war years, it was a common spectacle to see generals and leaders humiliating priests and seizing and plundering churches, which they would adapt as public offices or seats of state congresses or simply just tear down. The government's anti-religiousness climaxed with President Plutarco Elías Calles, a general with open communist sympathies.

With no counterweights, the state that emerged from the Mexican Revolution tried to put religious institutions under dictatorial control. This produced one of the most little-known episodes in the history of Mexico, one that, for many years, the state tried to slide under the rug: the Cristero War, a kind of counter-revolution that the new state never suspected could happen. The Cristero War, also known as La

Cristiada, ravaged the whole center of the country. The Constitution of 1917 restricted religious education, outlawed monastic orders, banned worship outside churches, and turned church property over to the ownership of the state. Further legal measures by the Calles administration gave the government the authority to determine the number of clergy officials in each state and prohibited religious publications, priestly celibacy, and monastic life, among other harsh measures. In those days, government forces stormed many churches on the pretext that they were not fulfilling the law, and they expelled nuns, priests, and bishops from the country. In some states, such as Tabasco, the governors forced the priests to marry.

When the Church responded with the announcement that it would suspend worship as a protest, Calles was pleased because he was sure that the measure would ultimately destroy the Catholic Church. At the same time, the most anticlerical president ever became active in religion; however, it was not Catholicism. Calles supported a schismatic movement to create a Mexican Catholic Apostolic Church, whose head was a rebel bishop named Joaquín Pérez. The proposed Church would not depend on the Vatican, and its highest authority would be Joaquín "the Patriarch" Pérez.

Calles also responded to the strike of public worship with the banning of private worship; this unprecedented measure, reminiscent of Christian persecution in ancient times, effectively made religion illegal. Thousands of people went to churches to receive the sacrament that, in a matter of days, would be grounds for imprisonment. Thousands of children were baptized, Masses were celebrated continuously for days, and an archbishop fainted from exhaustion after confirming five thousand people in a single day. The so-called Calles Law came in full force on August 1ˢᵗ, 1926, and the government sent its forces to seal the doors of the churches and seize their inventories, and then closed confessional schools, as well as convents and monasteries. Many Catholics protested. The government responded by imprisoning more priests. In 1927, Father

Francisco Vera was arrested for celebrating Mass and taken to the firing squad. The general who ordered the execution of Father Vera, who stood in his full attire with hands clasped in a sign of prayer before the four-men firing squad, took an infamous photo of the execution and sent it to President Calles, who, in turn, passed it to the press. Dismissed by intellectuals and the state as a reactionary movement to the progressive Mexican Revolution, the Cristero War had indeed been spawned by a genuine and bloody religious persecution.

Mexicans to this day remember tales told by their grandparents about families hiding priests and nuns in their attics and cellars for years to save them from arrest, deportation, or execution by firing squad. The religious war lasted from 1926 to 1929. Catholic peasants of the states of Guanajuato, Zacatecas, Aguascalientes, Jalisco, and Colima formed resistance groups with no experience, especially compared to the 70,000-men federal army, fresh from the Mexican Revolution. The Cristeros rode in groups of fifty to one hundred men, fighting local wars completely unprepared, only to be massacred. But things soon changed.

It was during the Cristero War that the government first used aviation for military purposes, even bombarding the famous sculpture of Christ the King in Guanajuato. In a year, however, the Cristero forces reached twenty thousand combatants. Women played an important role in the war. While in the Mexican Revolution, their role had been to cook for the troops, during the Cristiada, they served as spies, propagandists, logistics, and resistance. When the army was going to seize a church, women usually occupied it while the men defended the surroundings. In 1927, the women also entered into combat when the Joan of Arc Brigade was established, named after the maid of Orléans, France, who had just been canonized in Rome. The Joan of Arc Brigade consisted of 650 women who, although they did not take up arms, did war work. They had ranks of general, colonel, and captain, and they controlled ammunition, weapons, medical assistance, and did espionage work. The brigade was composed mostly of teenage women carrying weapons and ammunition to the battlefields, putting their lives at risk.

In the beginning, the Cristero movement suffered from the lack of a leading figure or central command until Enrique Gorostieta, a soldier who had fought in the Mexican Revolution, emerged and brought organization and unity to an effort that was local and split up. The movement that the government initially criticized and derided as a phony revolution now deserved not only their concern but also the Vatican's and the rest of the world. The Cristeros were never a real threat to the government, as they could not aspire to overthrow the regime. This was a movement located in central Mexico, and the men had no military training and many internal divisions. And they certainly did not have the support of the Church or the Vatican, at least officially.

In 1928, General Álvaro Obregón was reelected to the presidency. When he was celebrating his victory in a restaurant with friends and allies, a young Catholic man posing as a cartoonist approached and asked him if he could draw a portrait. President-elect Obregón agreed, saw the cartoon and, laughing, passed it among those present. Then the young man pulled out a gun and emptied his gun with six shots. The officers tried to execute him right there, but a person stopped them, saying that it was necessary to know who had sent him. The young man was a religious fanatic who, in his statement, said he had done it "so that Christ our Lord can reign in Mexico." The Church condemned the killing, and the murderer was executed by a firing squad in 1929. Before he was shot, he extended his arms to form the cross and died without being able to say, like all the Cristeros during the war, "Long live Christ the King." José de León Toral, the confessed assassin, became a martyr for some Cristeros.

The movement, crossed out as a fabricated reactionary movement by the revolutionary generation of 1910, became important enough to alarm global public opinion and to pressure the government and the Church to reach an agreement. In 1928, Pope Pius XI sent a letter to Mexican Catholics asking them to have trust, as negotiations were ongoing. In 1929, when the Cristero forces had already reached fifty thousand people, and countless combatants and priests lay in their graves, representatives of the Vatican met with the Mexican clergy and the United States ambassador, Dwight W. Morrow. President Calles, in the last year of his tenure, also met with representatives of the Mexican and international Church, as well as Ambassador Morrow, to try to attain a solution. In June, the government and the Church signed a peace agreement, and an unspoken promise was reached not to apply the anticlerical laws. The Mexican Church resumed worship in the Basilica of Guadalupe, under the image that was believed to be miraculous since the colonial period, the image that had mobilized Mexicans at different times to rebel against injustice. The Cristero combatants, who were required to present themselves in order to deliver their weapons and receive safe passage, disbanded and vanished as they had come, without notifying anyone, and returned to their ranches and towns in central Mexico. The women renovated many ruined churches, confident that their holy war had come to an end.

The relations between the Church and the state would remain tense for the rest of the century. In the next decade, the same circumstances recurred, and a second and shorter Cristiada swept the central part of the country. As the 1940s entered, President Manuel Ávila Camacho apparently settled the matter when he declared that he was a Catholic. When Ávila said, "I am a believer," he was the first Mexican president since the Mexican Revolution to openly admit it. But the world was going to take a turn with World War II, and Mexico's priorities, like those of the rest of the world, would change radically. Unlike the First World War, this time Mexico would need to make a decision that would define its future forever. Would it side with the Allies or with the Axis?

Chapter 10 – The Second World War and the Mexican Miracle

Lázaro Cárdenas, perhaps the most popular and respected president in Mexico's history, came to the presidency with a pacified country, but the countryside was ruined, and the peasant class was still waiting for the promises of the Mexican Revolution, land and freedom, to be fulfilled. Cárdenas carried out an agrarian reform as Zapata would have wanted, under which a total of eighteen million hectares would be distributed to the peasant communities under a property regime called *ejido*, which prevented the lands from being sold, bought, disposed of, or lost to debtors. Cárdenas also nationalized the oil industry at a critical time; it was 1938, a year before the beginning of the Second World War. At this time, the country had become a budding oil power, and its main clients, Great Britain and the United States, owned the facilities nationalized by the government. Upon hearing the news, they promoted an economic boycott to starve Mexico, and a few investors in those nations even called for a new intervention to compensate for the losses. But the beginning of World War II changed the whole scenario.

The Western powers were alarmed to see that Nazi Germany had not joined the boycott against Mexico. On the contrary, the Third

Reich sold Mexico the necessary chemicals to keep its oil industry running so they could sell the essential fuel to Führer Adolf Hitler. With the Anglo-Saxon embargo, Nazi Germany became the main buyer of Mexican oil. Britain and the United States realized that their small revenge had thrown Mexico into the Nazi sphere. Mexico passed from selling one million barrels of oil a year to the Third Reich to almost five million in 1939, the year of the invasion of Poland. It is entirely possible some blitzkrieg tanks that crushed the Polish villages were fueled by Mexican oil. Nazi Germany began to send spies and conspirators to Mexico, who carried out the essential task of sending sensitive information back about the United States while initiating an ideological struggle to cast all of Latin America to the Axis side. But Mexico kept a sound and clear-minded policy. When Hitler annexed Austria in 1938, beginning his expansionist policy that no one dared to criticize, Mexico was the only country in the world to protest against the *Anschluss.*

President Cárdenas got a secret report sent by his Ministry of Interior, officially informing him that there was a powerful Nazi network operating in the country. Until the end of his time in office, Cárdenas maintained his pro-democratic discourse but also neutrality in the war, as well as commercial ties with both sides.

By the end of 1940, with a presidential election approaching, the Nazi intervention in Mexico became intolerable for the United States, and it began to press Cárdenas. In 1941, the new president, Manuel Ávila Camacho, signed an agreement with the United States allowing it to use its air bases and supported a commercial treaty to sell oil again. This decision cost Mexico. In May of 1942, Germany bombed and sank several Mexican ships in the Gulf of Mexico in retaliation for selling fuel to the führer's enemy.

The first ship was *Potrero del Llano.* The boat was carrying 6,000 tons of oil and 35 crew members. Thirteen perished, including its captain, while the rest were rescued by an American ship. Some newspapers in Mexico reported that the Germans had exterminated the survivors struggling to stay afloat with submachine guns. The arrival of the corpses to Mexican territory deeply impacted the national mood, and more people were inclined to Mexico breaking its neutrality. In the following days, German submarines attacked more crafts. Finally, on May 28th, Mexico declared "a state of war" with the Axis powers. Although Mexico was the heir to a long tradition of bad American ambassadors, on that occasion, it got a shrewd visionary and an attentive ambassador who was concerned for the future of Mexico. George Messersmith saw the convenience not only of Mexico declaring war and supporting the US with raw materials and men to harvest their fields but also its ability to send a combat force to the war front. It would be the first time in the country's history. To achieve this, Messersmith was going to have to pass through a maze of interests, opposition, and bureaucracy.

For the Mexicans themselves, it was a surprise to learn that this time their country was on the same side as the United States. There was still much resentment one hundred years after the war and the loss of its northern territory. The Mexican-American historian and writer for *The New York Times* Anita Brenner told how the news was received in the town of San Andrés. People were enjoying the evening on the plaza benches when the radio announced that Mexico was at war yet again. The people shouted, "*Viva México!* Death to the *gringos!*" (*gringos* referring to the Americans) and even "*Viva la Revolución!*" Suddenly, the town's telegrapher interrupted the jubilant exclamations. "Idiots! Imbeciles!" he said. "We're against Germany! ... Don't you understand the Americans are on our side? We´re fighting Fascism!" On the other side of the crowd, where the women were, an old, cracked voice cried, "God preserve us! Who would have ever told me that I would come to be praying for *gringos...!*"

The Aztec Eagles

Thanks to the work of Ambassador Messersmith in Mexico and the US, both presidents agreed on the convenience of Mexico participating, albeit symbolically, with an infantry division or an air combat squad. Ávila Camacho and Franklin D. Roosevelt agreed that it would be best to send a squad of fighter planes to General Douglas MacArthur, who was in the Pacific at the time. Air squadrons presented fewer human casualties and had a superior destruction capacity. The fighter squadrons also constituted the first line of attack to destroy military targets, force the enemy to flee, and clear the way for ground troops. Despite their small size in comparison with units fighting on the ground, the thirty-pilot squadrons were a significant factor on the Pacific front, which was ultimately the last stage of the Second World War. In 1944, Mexico finally sent their group of thirty pilots for training in the United States to fight against Japan in the liberation of the Philippines. The men of the 201st Fighter Squadron, also known as the Aztec Eagles, arrived in Manila in the nick of time on April 30th, 1945, as the war was coming to a close.

At first, when they arrived at the air base near Manila, the Mexicans received cold and even hostile treatment from the Americans, who felt that the "petite" pilots—as they were much shorter than the Marines—were only going to get in the way. Before going into combat, spirits were heated and near fistfights. It was just the tension before the action. The Aztec Eagles finally received the order to board their planes in May 1945 and receive their baptism of fire. Before doing so, they wrote letters home. Although we now know that the Second World War would last less than four more months, at the time, the Allies were looking forward to a prolonged and costly war in terms of human lives, as Japan had sworn it would never surrender.

Back home in Mexico, an excited and nervous press reported that the Mexicans had just entered into combat in the Philippines against Japanese units. Twenty aircraft from the 201st Squadron, under the orders of Captain Radamés Gaxiola, took part in the operation, bombing and gunning tanks and trucks on the island of Luzon. The Japanese responded with anti-aircraft fire. The first casualty came in

June when 22-year-old pilot Fausto Vega Santander died during a difficult mission against a Japanese ammunition depot. In addition to anti-aircraft fire, the Japanese had three natural defenses in the form of high cliffs; the only possible approach was from the sea and through a narrow opening. The 201ª Squadron's commander suggested that the only way to destroy the depot was to dive-bomb it from a very high altitude, which was virtually a suicide mission. The Mexicans succeeded where other Allied pilots had failed, but the act also cost Mexico its first pilot overseas.

The 201ª Squadron accumulated 785 defensive missions and six offensive missions in the Philippines and Taiwan, and it is calculated that they eliminated, nullified, or expelled around thirty thousand Japanese soldiers over two months. But Mexico's role in World War II was more symbolic than real. Mexico only lost five pilots, which is a footnote compared to the over 400,000 American or the almost nine million Russian casualties. The 201ª Squadron's greatest triumph was not achieved in the airspace of the Far East but in the diplomatic realm. Thanks to its participation, a new era of international relations began between Mexico and the United States, two countries that had been hostile and distrustful toward each other since basically forever. It also allowed the former to be on the side of the winners in the Second World War, and it became a founding member of the United Nations.

The Northward Migration

The Second World War brought a demographic phenomenon that helps to explain present-day Mexico: the migration of peasants and unskilled workers to the United States. Since the Mexican Revolution, some Mexicans had emigrated north to escape violence. The Great Depression of the 1930s saw the mass deportation of Mexicans, including those families who had lived on the north side of the Rio Grande since before the war with the United States, the so-called Chicanos. But the migration northward in large numbers began in the 1940s. Contrary to what many believe, it was the United

States who first asked Mexico to send workers to harvest its fields because hands and arms were lacking for agriculture. In 1942, in the first harvest after the attack on Pearl Harbor, California farmers expressed their concern to the government that there would be a shortage of workers in the fields and requested that their government import one hundred thousand Mexican workers.

The governments, represented by Franklin D. Roosevelt and Manuel Ávila Camacho, signed an urgent agreement known as the Bracero Program, *bracero* being a Spanish word meaning a man who works with his arms. The program was given a limited duration and would last only during the war years. Mexico even had the luxury of establishing conditions in order to send its peasants: migrants would get roundtrip transportation from their towns to the harvest fields, they would be paid the same wage as the Americans who did the same work, and they would receive protection and essential healthcare. In the first year of the Bracero Program, four thousand Mexican workers entered the United States with all benefits. Only one year later, the number increased to 44,000 and then 62,000 in the last year of World War II. The program was too favorable for the business of US farmers, who demanded that the binational agreement continue for a few more years. The Bracero Program came to legally admit up to 200,000 workers per year in the 1950s, not counting those who were attracted to agricultural companies outside the institutional channels; those workers received lower salaries. In 1956, the number of temporary and legal agricultural workers in the United States reached a record high of 450,000 people. American agricultural workers had the possibility to leave their jobs in the countryside to go look for urban jobs, which, in turn, led to greater demand for agricultural workers and greater migration of Mexican peasants. The flow continued for many years with the tacit approval of the US government and with poor conditions for Mexicans. In this way, a migration process from south to north started, and it continues today.

This demographic movement was also the origin of two developments that characterized the second half of the 20th century: the expansion of Mexican culture in the United States, mainly in Texas, California, and New Mexico; and the Chicano movement in the southern United States, where the figure of César Chávez, the son of poor Mexican migrants, is paramount. A former worker in the vineyards in California, Chávez fought for the dignification of Hispanic American farmworkers. Inspired by Gandhi and his techniques of nonviolence, such as civil resistance and fasting, Chávez first encouraged agricultural workers of Mexican origin to organize, to register to vote, to voice complaints, and to strike.

Initially, Chávez began to unionize the fields and orchards of California, where he issued a call to boycott grapes from the state, and his movement acquired such a force that it captured worldwide attention. Agricultural entrepreneurs ended up recognizing the union founded by Chávez, United Farm Workers. At a time when the West saw communism as the worst of evils, Chávez was being monitored by the FBI. "It is my deepest belief that only by giving our lives do we find life," he said once. "I am convinced that the truest act of courage, the strongest act of manliness is to sacrifice ourselves for others in a totally non-violent struggle for justice." César Chávez thus represents the best of the Mexican diaspora. He became an icon of the Mexican community in the United States and indirectly, thanks to his work for the empowerment of Chicanos, also became a factor in the emergence of this ethnic group as an important electoral political force.

Chapter 11 – End of Century Pangs

"We Mexicans, on the other hand, fight against imaginary entities, vestiges of the past or ghosts engendered by ourselves. They are impalpable and invincible because they are not outside us but within us."

—Nobel Prize Winner Octavio Paz

Mexico lived its golden age— "the Mexican miracle" as it was known throughout the world—in the 1950s and 1960s. For the first time since it stopped calling itself New Spain, the country was at peace, with economic growth, social peace, a healthy demographic expansion that began to populate the farthest corners of the country, and flourishing arts. A new appreciation for its pre-Hispanic past, as well as the archaeological works in Mexico City to dig up the ruins of Tenochtitlan and restoring the Mayan pyramids and temples in Yucatan, made Mexico one of the main tourist destinations. Great personalities visited Mexico for the first time, such as Dwight D. Eisenhower, John F. Kennedy, Charles de Gaulle, Josip Broz Tito, Queen Juliana of the Netherlands, and Akihito and Michiko, the rulers of Japan from 1989 to 2019 (although it should be noted they visited Japan in the 1960s). The new Basilica of Guadalupe was inaugurated, and the National Museum of Anthropology was the object of general admiration. How had Mexico achieved this miracle?

Post-war Mexico had adopted a plan of nationalist development. Its economic strategy was to adopt a protectionist policy with high import tariffs in order to develop its own industry. The government encouraged national investments and offered clear rules and reliability to investors. At the same time, a welfare state was created that offered workers free education, free healthcare, price controls, and the right to organize in exchange for discipline and loyalty to the post-revolutionary regime. This stage was known as "stabilizing development," and it allowed Mexican baby boomers to enjoy a period of unprecedented prosperity and stability. Economic growth was historic, reaching a yearly 6.8 percent on average. Industrial production also grew at a similar pace, and best of all, all of this was achieved without inflation. On the other hand, in a more subtle way, the government quickly and effectively suppressed any alteration of order.

But in the late 1960s, the model began to show its limitations. In 1968, when student protests broke out all over the world, and the press talked about the riots in Paris, the Mexican counterculture also aired its demands, and the students took the streets. Again, the student protests focused on the capital, and they quickly increased until they became alarming for the government. The pro-government press—practically all the newspapers—talked about a communist conspiracy.

A few days before the 1968 Summer Olympics were held in Mexico City, the government did the unthinkable. On October 2nd, dozens of tanks and five thousand soldiers stormed from all sides on a student demonstration that was protesting peacefully in the Tlatelolco Square and fired on approximately ten thousand students and others who attended the rally. The crowd panicked and started running over dead bodies. The assault on Tlatelolco left a death toll that has never been established since the government took care to buy the press, seize all photographic materials, and hide the dead. During the night, the fire department showered Tlatelolco Square with fire hoses to rinse the blood. Eyewitnesses and survivors estimate that up to five hundred people died that day.

The Tlatelolco massacre was not an isolated event. It was the climax of a series of protests and the manifestation of a visible malaise: the stabilizing development, with all its merits, had developed Mexico, but it had burnt out. The channels of participation in politics were closed, and although elections were held, democracy was fictitious, and the gap between rich and poor had widened. The student massacre was the drop that spilled the glass and the clearest sign that the long post-revolutionary state—represented by the state party, the Institutional Revolutionary Party (PRI)—had become a kind of "perfect dictatorship." Many of the disappointed and angry leaders of the student protests went underground, and during the next two decades, clandestine guerrilla movements surfaced in northern and southern Mexico. The government was implacable and adopted dirty war tactics against the most visible guerrilla factions. At the same time, the wealthy farmers in the south formed government-sponsored paramilitary groups to suppress any indigenous resistance. More slowly and discreetly, another movement was gradually maturing, which would make its appearance two decades later.

The government tried to make a left turn toward a welfare state to help fix the acute social lags, and it laid the foundations for a new development model supported by a large treasure that had been literally hidden underground: its immense oil reserves. At the beginning of the 1980s, Mexico was one of the largest oil producers in the world. It had such an influence in the market that it constituted a power similar to that of OPEC. But the temporary bonanza came with an expensive bill. The price of oil suddenly collapsed from 125 dollars per barrel in 1980 to 64 dollars in 1985. For a country like

Mexico, which had borrowed extensively to develop its oil industry and tied its economy to the so-called "black gold," the price drop could only mean problems. The 1980s was the "lost decade," not only for Mexico but for Latin America. Mexico renegotiated its foreign debt and adopted a more open and liberal economic model based not only on oil exports but on a more diversified industry and foreign trade. President Carlos Salinas de Gortari, a reformer, signed a free trade agreement with the United States and Canada, raising the question among international analysts whether North America would become an economic bloc in the style of the European Union. But it was too late. A voice from the past, which emerged from the southern mountains, reminded the world that the indigenous cause was far from being resolved.

The Zapatistas

Seventy-five years after the death of Emiliano Zapata, the idolized peasant freedom fighter of 1910, the indigenous people of the south declared war on the Mexican government, claiming Zapata's legacy. The indigenous armies with obsolete weapons and their faces covered with handkerchiefs took the town of San Cristóbal de las Casas on January 1st, 1994, the same day the North American Free Trade Agreement (NAFTA) went into effect. In the early hours, they released indigenous prisoners and destroyed land titles. The decision to begin their rebellion in San Cristóbal was a fine irony: as recently as the decade of the 1950s, Native Americans were not allowed to enter the city, which was a picturesque tourist destination. The date chosen was also a blunt message. While the government looked outside, pretending to be a first-world country with the signing of NAFTA, the Zapatista Army of National Liberation was a reminder that the Native Americans in Mexico were still there. On January 1st, the Zapatista forces, which were formed by fighters of the Tzotzil, Tzeltal, Tojolab'al, and Ch'ol ethnic groups, took the other six villages in the San Cristóbal region with rifles, machetes, and knives. They wore brown shirts, green pants, and rubber boots. Some brought backpacks and sophisticated firearms, while others carried wooden rifles painted with shoe grease.

In a statement that surprised the world, the Zapatistas announced their intention to march to Mexico City to defeat the federal army and liberate cities. They accused all of the previous governments of practicing an undeclared genocidal war against indigenous peoples, without caring that they were "starving and dying of curable diseases, not caring that we have nothing, absolutely nothing, not a decent roof, no land, no work, no health, no food, no education." At the head of the uprising was an anonymous character with a pipe and a ski mask, Rafael Sebastián Guillén Vicente, although his eyes did not look indigenous. His attire was completed by a bandolier crossing his chest, a submachine gun, a small pipe in his mouth, and a way of communicating that demonstrated high education. Guillén, better known as Subcomandante Marcos, had lived for decades in the mountains of Mexico, organizing the rebellion. "Forgive the inconvenience," the Zapatista leader told an angry tour guide who complained that he had to take his group to the ruins of Palenque, "but this is a revolution."

Marcos was not exaggerating in his statement. Half of the indigenous population of Chiapas, which was rich in natural resources but the second poorest state in the republic, had no income at all. The natives, who had once populated the entire territory, had been withdrawing toward the south over the last five centuries. The mountainous terrain of Chiapas, which was difficult to exploit and traverse, accommodated most of the country's indigenous peoples. The Zapatistas, of which approximately one-third were armed indigenous women, were poor, low in number — having approximately three thousand troops—and clearly did not pose a risk to the government, but President Carlos Salinas, nevertheless, decided to respond brutally. Firstly, the government sowed the idea that the Zapatistas were foreign guerrillas, terrorists, or drug traffickers, but they weren't actually any of those.

A column of eight hundred soldiers arrived in the town of Ocosingo in the afternoon of January 2nd, 1994. Ocosingo is a town in the mountains with twelve thousand inhabitants near the border of Guatemala. The Zapatistas had pulled out of most of the towns after the arrival of the army but not Ocosingo. They were concentrated in the market, where a battle ensued that lasted all night. On January 3rd, the army decided to take the market by storm. With instructions from the higher command to have no second thoughts about summary executions, the federal troops raided the city center. Later, the fight continued house by house. At night, the Zapatistas tried to break the siege by concentrating their forces on a single point and tried to reach a hill that would take them back to the jungle, but they were unprepared. The Ocosingo massacre reverberated worldwide. To recover other towns that could not be seized by ground forces, the president approved the use of the Mexican Air Force. Photographs of indigenous men and women killed in their own lands traveled the world, despite the army's efforts to clear the battlefield, and it had a shattering media effect against the Mexican government. The images are chilling, as if they were taken from a barbaric past. The confrontations continued for twelve days and ended when the government recovered the occupied towns, with hundreds of Zapatistas dead. The indigenous peoples were driven back to the jungle of Chiapas, and President Carlos Salinas assured the nation that the government was in control.

However, Salinas had made a terrible miscalculation. The images of the brief war against the native peoples impacted large sectors of Mexican society. Ten days after the start of the conflict, more than one hundred thousand people demonstrated in Mexico City in support of the Zapatistas. The president flinched. The Native Americans had awakened, once again, international consciousness and shaken Mexican society. The just nature of their demands called worldwide attention. Soon, thousands of international observers arrived. In a matter of weeks, the Zapatista rebellion was one of the most famous social movements in the world and had awakened an unexpected level of solidarity. "We did not go to war on January 1 to kill, or to have them kill us. We went to make ourselves heard," said Marcos, and he had accomplished just that.

The Mexican government was the first to be surprised by the uprising and the degree of attention it gained internationally, especially the figure of the enigmatic Subcomandante Marcos, who became a celebrity among intellectuals around the world. A ceasefire was declared, and a pardon was offered by the government. "What are they going to pardon us for?" the hooded leader asked in a new statement. "For not dying of hunger? For not accepting our misery in silence? For not humbly accepting the huge historic burden of disdain and abandonment? For having risen up in arms when we found all other paths closed? For having shown the country and the whole world that human dignity still exists and is in the hearts of the most impoverished inhabitants? For having made careful preparations before beginning our fight? For having brought guns to battle instead of bows and arrows? For being mostly Indigenous? Who should ask for forgiveness and who can grant it? Those who, for years and years, sat before a full table and satiated themselves while we sat with death, as such a daily factor in our lives that we stopped even fearing it?"

Soon, the peace negotiations began. The bishop of San Cristóbal, Samuel Ruiz, a respected figure that the rebels trusted and a priest identified with liberation theology, acted as a mediator. The Zapatistas demanded a new relationship between the state and the indigenous peoples. The San Andrés Accords proposed the right to autonomy of the indigenous peoples, meaning they would decide how to organize themselves politically, socially, economically, and culturally. They asked the state to set up mechanisms to guarantee conditions that would allow them to satisfactorily accomplish their nourishment, health, and housing. In their view, Mexico's policy for Native Americans should set up priority programs for the improvement of health and nourishment of children, as well as programs for the training of women. The administration of the new president, Ernesto Zedillo, could accept these social demands, but the heart of the San Andrés Accords—autonomy—was too much for a government that perhaps feared losing Chiapas, as it had already once happened in the 19th century. This would have been the first step toward Mexico's "balkanization," a concern no doubt inferred from the Yugoslav Wars, which at that time was at its peak.

In February 1995, the government made a surprise counterattack, violating the conditions of the ceasefire. The government also disclosed the identity of Subcomandante Marcos, who was a former student of philosophy at Mexico City's UNAM (National Autonomous University of Mexico), and recovered the Zapatista territory by force. In the early hours of February 9th, the army broke the Native American positions with planes, helicopters, and soldiers on foot, demolishing houses, killing farm animals, and destroying crops. The inhabitants, fearing reprisals, left the villages and took refuge in the mountains, including children. Zedillo delivered a triumphal address on national television, but the government strategy failed again. By showing Marcos's face on television without his mask, the president hoped to demystify the Subcomandante's aura and make him lose social support. But the incursion had just the opposite effect. In the face of new aggression, more mass protests followed, especially in Mexico City, the place of old Tenochtitlan, where a large crowd assembled wearing ski masks, shouting in solidarity, "We are all Marcos!"

The scene could not be more symbolic. After five hundred years, in the same place where the Aztec Empire had come to an end, people reunited once again to recognize Mexico's historical debt and perhaps feel a little guilt toward those who had been there first.

Conclusion: Mexico

Benito Juárez, universally acclaimed as one of the best, if not the best, president of Mexico, once said, "Why is Mexico, my country, so strange that it is formed, half and half, of an inexhaustible source of tenderness and a deep well of bestiality?" Did Juárez have the Mexican flag in mind when he said this, where a noble eagle and a snake fight to death eternally, the symbol of two opposing forces, one from heaven and another from the earth?

Mexico is a country of contrasts, from its geography to its people. Its history is one of encounter and conflict, of triumphs that become failures once they display their limitations to solve the needs of a society, a society that was born from one of those encounters, a violent one between Montezuma and Hernán Cortés. In 1810, the independence started by fathers Miguel Hidalgo and José María Morelos gave rise to a country that became addicted to solving its problems with coups and proclamations. The ardor of the 19th-century Liberals to create an egalitarian society led them to excesses that provoked an equally bitter reaction, which led to France's intervention and a tragic monarchy. The Mexican Revolution of 1910, which fought for agrarian reform and social justice, ended up being authoritarian and anticlerical, engendering first the Cristero War and then the broad social unrest of the 1960s. Therefore, it is only appropriate to say that today's Mexico, a 200-year-old independent country with ancient roots, is still looking for that long-awaited balance and definitive encounter. "Mexico is a beautiful country, one of the most beautiful on Earth," wrote the intellectual Jesús Silva-Herzog, "but it is still under construction, and what matters most is to finish the job, and the sooner the better."

However, not everything has been violent. From these encounters between races, cultures, and ideas, so often bloody, Mexico has managed to get the best out of its men and women, who have given the world many contributions. Although civilization might be possible without them, no one would want to live in a world without them. The Maya invented the zero around 350 BCE and used it as a placeholder in their complex calendars; also—although other countries would wince at this statement—they invented football (soccer for those American readers) or at least a very similar game. The Aztecs were the first civilization in the world to grant universal and free education, regardless of age, class, or gender in a world where, until recently, school was reserved for the rich and noble. The Aztecs were also the creators of the first zoo in the Americas.

Many delicacies, such as chocolate, tequila, avocado, corn tortillas, and popcorn, were all born in Mexico. The world not only fell in love with chocolate, but other cultures decided to preserve its original name in the Nahuatl language: chocolate in English, *sokoláta* in Greek, *čokoláda* in Czech, *shukulata* in Arabic, and *shukuledi* in Zulu. In the case of tortillas, the basic element of the famous taco, there is evidence that it was prepared in Oaxaca three thousand years ago; when it comes to the avocado, the base of the well-known guacamole, there is evidence that it was consumed ten thousand years ago in the state of Puebla. Not in vain, Mexican cuisine is one of the three cuisines in all the world—along with French and Japanese—that is considered as Intangible Cultural Heritage by UNESCO.

The color television was developed by electrical engineer Guillermo González Camarena when he was 23. The contraceptive pill was synthesized by chemist Luis Ernesto Miramontes Cárdenas. In the field of science, Mario Molina, the winner of the Nobel Prize in 1995, demonstrated the mechanism by which the ozone layer is destroyed and noted the thinning of the layer in Antarctica, creating global awareness of the danger of CFCs.

As the 21st century sets in, new historical challenges open for Mexico: the threat of drug trafficking, the problem of migration with the United States, and addressing its regional and economic inequalities, all problems that remain endemic. But new opportunities will also open up in the next years. Mexico might have a leadership position in Latin America, and in the distant future, it will possibly witness, along with its northern neighbor, the birth of a new third country between Mexico and the United States that futurologists call MexAmerica, for lack of a better name.

Mexicans are widely known as hospitable and affectionate to visitors and strangers. "Mexico has a place for foreigners, it has a strange melody," said artist Chavela Vargas, who, although born in Costa Rica, was a self-proclaimed Mexican. "To say Mexico is to say something sweet, sweet Mexico. Mexico is the divine word, the magic word, the wise word. It is about its sound and color that appears in our minds when we say it. It is a smell." If we add Mexico's enormous biodiversity—the territory is home to almost 70 percent of the world's variety of plants and animals—and archeological treasures to the mixture, it is not surprising that it is today the sixth most visited country in the world. And if traveling around its lands makes it an unforgettable and surprising experience for strangers, no less fascinating is the complex and dramatic history of a nation where one of the first civilizations of the planet surged, a people of astronomers and warriors. A history that includes the meeting between Cortés and Montezuma, where globalization really began. With 130 million people, it is, in every sense, a place so recognizable that one can clearly see it from space, a horn with two peninsulas like stretched hands surrounded, just as in ancient times, by azure waters. Mexicans have a saying for that. "They don't come any better than Mexico." Or in Spanish, "*Como México no hay dos.*"

Part 2: THE MEXICAN REVOLUTION

A Captivating Guide to the Mexican Civil War and How Pancho Villa and Emiliano Zapata Impacted Mexico

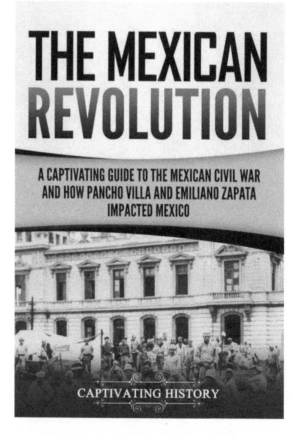

Introduction

The Mexican Revolution was a defining moment of the 20th century. The Mexican fight for democracy, equality, and justice sent shockwaves around the world. No other episode in its history has left a deeper mark. It is a three-act drama full of politics, persecution, and war, not to mention earthquakes, signs in the sky, and even spiritualist sessions, while being populated by larger-than-life villains, international spies, and the universally known figures of Pancho Villa and Emiliano Zapata. In fact, our modern idea of "revolution" owes much to what happened in this country between 1910 and 1920.

Although the uprisings of the oppressed classes have occurred since antiquity, Mexico in the 20th century is a unique case—this was the first triumphant popular revolution that, unlike others, was able to establish a popular government that carried out extensive social transformations without resorting to state terror, as was the case in the Soviet Union and China. It integrated marginalized groups into national life, and it gave birth to a refurbished nation, where, for a hundred years, there has not been a new coup d'état, a problem that devastated other Latin American countries during the 20th century. In a way, the course of the First World War was defined through Mexico, and the ideological expressions that emerged during that decade, such as the Plan of Ayala and the 1917 Constitution, influenced movements as far away as the Russian Revolution, the Republic of Weimar, and the Zapatista uprising of 1994. Several Central American insurrections in the last quarter of the 20th century owe much to its influence.

Hence, the Mexican Revolution has been an inexhaustible well for historians and novelists. Books in various languages could fill a large library, from the first accounts when the roar of the cannons had barely died down to the third decade of the 21st century, which has already seen the appearance of new volumes and biographies. The books entitled "A Short History..." of the Mexican Revolution, or something of the like, are legion. One of the most interesting aspects of the Mexican Revolution is that it was one of the first wars in the world to be widely documented through photography and cinema. Emiliano Zapata, in the imagination of the inhabitants of Mexico City, was the "Mexican Attila," a savage from the mountains leading hordes of bandits who raped and destroyed, which is something that the press of the capital deliberately fabricated. When Zapata's peasant army finally marched into the city, the citizens found that the reality was quite different.

Finally, the Mexican Revolution was not just one more war in a long list but an almost genetic transformation of the nation that, in its aftermath, was able to create a cultural and intellectual movement that formed the identity of what is now recognized as typically "Mexican," such as Diego Rivera's murals and Saturnino Herrán's paintings, the music of Manuel M. Ponce, and the novels of Mariano Azuela.

This book by *Captivating History* appears in the year of the hundredth anniversary of the end of the Mexican Revolution and is a handy guide for the neophyte reader who wants to learn everything from scratch.

Chapter 1 – The Comet

"By the time the comet appears on the western horizon, after May 20, it will present a spectacle so magnificent and astonishing that we must remember it as one of the great events of our lives, and in later years we will speak to our grandchildren of the great year of 1910."

El Faro, April 15, 1910, a few months before the Mexican Revolution began

A small comet popped up in the sky of Mexico City in the early hours before dawn. It flew across the winter firmament, which at that time was particularly bright and clear. It was hardly a blotch in the sky. At first, only the astronomers—a profession that Mexico had had since the time of the Mayas—showed interest in the return of Halley's Comet. But 1910 was going to be a spectacular sighting. By the beginning of May, the star and its tail crossed the vault of heaven from horizon to horizon, and it was visible even at midday. Even in our times, the appearance of a comet can cause anxiety in some people. It was no wonder that at the dawn of the 20th century, it was seen as an ominous sign by most Mexicans, those rural people who worked from sunrise to sunset and who, for the most part, were poor and illiterate. The older men and women said that it was a sign that a calamity was coming, just as in ancient times when a comet had announced the fall of Montezuma's empire before the arrival of the Spaniards.

In the spring of 1910, panic spread, not only among the poor and illiterate, when the scientific community announced that in mid-May, Earth would pass through the gaseous tail of the comet. It is unclear where the pernicious rumor started, which was widely reproduced in the newspapers of the time, that Halley's *cauda* (Latin for "tail") contained poisonous cyanogen gas that would exterminate all humanity. The news spread like a pandemic, although the most serious scientists reported that this would not be the case—some said that the tail would only give people the effect of laughing gas and that, in the worst-case scenario, humanity would just be laughing their brains out during the encounter.

But it was too late. By then, those who knew how natural phenomena worked said that the comet would collide with Earth, that the tail was toxic, or that gravitational forces would create destructive tides in every continent. Those who did not know about physics simply had a feeling that the wandering star was an omen and that a major affliction was going to fall on Mexico. Maybe a great war. Or the plague. On the day set for the encounter between the planet and the comet, on May 18th, to be precise, the churches across Mexico were crowded with people seeking confession, believing that the end was near. But as the parishioners lined up in front of the confessionals, surely no one knew that the danger had, in fact, already passed. At nine o'clock in the morning, without anyone noticing, the world passed through the tail of the most famous comet in history. On May 19th, the newspapers reported with relief that the predictions had failed. But the older men and women knew better.

Ten years after the comet, in 1920, the date when most historians place the end of the Mexican Revolution, 10 to 20 percent of the Mexicans had died, and little was left of that 19th-century country, which had seen Halley's Comet with astonished eyes. Its fields, haciendas, and villages were semi-destroyed, the bulletproof adobe walls of the houses punctured with holes, and people trembled at the sight of a group of men on horseback. Bridges, roads, and telegraph poles were shattered in many places. Even worse, almost every single family had at least one member missing due to some battle, the hundreds of executions that took place, thousands of self-exiles, women being seized by parties of horsemen, or deaths from disease and hunger. Between two to three million people, including both military and civilian statistics, had died, and blood soaked the fields in the north, center, and south of the country. This is a shocking figure if one considers that this number represented around 20 percent of the population at that time. Several presidents had passed through the National Palace in Mexico City, including one whose tenure only lasted 45 minutes, and the newspapers had reported two assassinations. It was not the tail of a comet that swept Mexico but rather a wind saturated with the voices of indignation, rage, criticism, and, above all, the demand for justice.

A revolution that had timidly begun as a democratic movement became a major economic and social upheaval that changed the face of the country. Ten years after Halley's Comet, a traveler would have seen a different Mexico. For a decade, the world watched the Mexican Revolution closely, the first important war to be extensively photographed, filmed, and reported on. In that time, from 1910 to 1920, Mexico had also gone through two invasions by the United States and became involved in a diplomatic affair with Germany that launched America into the First World War.

The storm that swept Mexico also ousted the old oligarchy and its army, built the foundations of government to end the servitude of the workers, and created the opportunity to redefine Mexico as a more egalitarian society. Even though it was half destroyed and still smelling of gunpowder, travelers who visited the country in 1920 would have noticed extensive devastation and a people fed up with the war but also something impalpable: the Mexican Revolution, with its two million deaths, had marked the route that would guide Mexico through the rest of the 20th century toward an ample agrarian reform, a popular and nationalist state, and, after a hundred years, a country that could, at last, aspire to live in peace.

But what had caused such a storm when no one could imagine in 1910 that a popular uprising—let alone a nationwide full-blown revolution—could take place in Mexico?

* * *

The year 1910 was marked by celebrations. The government spared no expense to celebrate the hundredth anniversary of the Mexican War of Independence of 1810. In control of the presidency was Porfirio Díaz, an old soldier who had fought against the French in the famous battle of Cinco de Mayo in Puebla, and he had ruled the country with a heavy hand for more than thirty years. For the centennial celebrations, he invited foreign representatives from every corner of the world to see a revamped Mexico City, complete with new monuments reminiscent of national glories, palaces, public facilities, and the jewel of the city—the new mercury streetlights. At the National Palace, there were lavish receptions with Mexican waitresses perfectly chosen to pass as foreigners—namely as blondes. A monument to George Washington was unveiled at one of them, and on September 16th, on Independence Day, the people behind the police lines marveled at a splendid parade with cars and floats that showed the history of Mexico, from Emperor Moctezuma and the great Tenochtitlán to the fight for independence and effigies of past heroes. In Chapultepec Forest, a new lake was inaugurated, and the people witnessed the march of foreign troops saluting Mexico, even France's *Pantalons Rouges*, against whom President Díaz had fought on Cinco de Mayo. The French envoy had a token of admiration and friendship for the old dictator, as he returned the keys of Mexico City, which his predecessor had received from Díaz's enemies in 1863. On September 23rd, which many considered the high point of the celebrations, a lavish dance was held at the National Palace, with 2,000 guests in attendance from all over the world. "I look at Porfirio Diaz, the President of Mexico, as one of the greatest men to be held up for the hero-worship of mankind," said US Secretary of State Elihu Root.

All of this happened in Mexico City, a very small portion of the national territory. But just as a hot air balloon floats up to discover the fields and small towns beyond, the attentive traveler could see, as he moved away from the big city, that Mexico was far from being Díaz's paradise of "Order and Progress," where foreign representatives toasted champagne in cut-glass wineglasses.

Chapter 2 – The Strong Man of the Americas

"Revolution *(noun)* – A major, sudden, and hence typically violent alteration in government and in related associations and structures. / A challenge to the established political order and the eventual establishment of a new order radically different from the preceding one."

—Encyclopedia Britannica

"I don't need lawyers. I need farmhands."

—Luis Terrazas, the richest landowner in Mexico, when they told him they wanted to put schools in his haciendas.

In his youth, Porfirio Díaz had been the hero of Mexico. When France invaded Mexico in 1862, seeking to establish a monarchy, Díaz was a spirited young general who showed heroic behavior in the famous battle of Cinco de Mayo, which is the most popular Mexican holiday in the world, though not in Mexico. After the French were defeated on the outskirts of Puebla, General Díaz chased them with his cavalry to finish them off, despite orders from his commanding general, Ignacio Zaragoza, to leave off. Díaz's comrades were able to make him come back only when Zaragoza threatened to sanction him. Five years later, after the fall of the monarchy of Maximilian of

Habsburg, Díaz had the glory of capturing the capital and marching into Mexico City, an event known as the Reestablishment of the Republic. Later, in 1877, Díaz became the president of the country he had helped save, and except for a brief interim of four years, he ruled Mexico for three decades without interruption under democratic appearances. He organized elections, but he had dismantled the opposition, eliminated his political rivals, put his friends in Congress and state governorships, and won election after election.

Porfirio Díaz is a controversial character in Mexico. Until recently, he was officially the villain of the story, but in recent years, historians have vindicated him to some degree. Díaz was a man of his time. As the president of a country destabilized by a series of coups and incessant local revolts, which threatened to dismember the nation, he managed to finally cut the cycle of coups and local guerrillas, giving Mexico a stability it had never known. During his tenure, known as the Porfiriato, foreign investment flowed into the country, and necessary infrastructure was built, especially railways, roads, and telegraphs. When Díaz took over Mexico, the country had 640 kilometers (almost 400 miles) of railroad tracks. In 1910, at the end of his term, there were almost 20,000 kilometers (close to 12,430 miles) of tracks, which was enough to get from Mexico City to Moscow and back. Before his time, Mexico was a collection of disconnected regions, which, thanks to the railroad, began to feel united and form something more like a nation. Foreign investment, especially American, developed mines and textile industries and exported agriculture, such as coffee, sugar, and henequen. For the first time, there was readily available employment, and real wages increased in one generation. Díaz paid off Mexico's foreign debt, something that had caused Mexico many headaches and foreign interventions in the past, and pacified the troubled areas of the Yucatan Peninsula and the northern border states, which had been devastated throughout the 19th century by the Apache incursions and other ethnic groups. In the international arena, Mexico joined globalization and established good diplomatic relations with powers from around the world. On each one of his birthdays, Díaz received congratulations from the Kaiser, the president of the United States, and the European monarchs. Don Porfirio was the first to meet with a president of the United States, William Taft, in El Paso-Ciudad Juárez. "You are, to my knowledge," said the old general to his chunky neighbor, "the first US premier to visit this land." For all these reasons, Díaz was called the Strong Man of the Americas.

But that prosperity was built upon impoverished and dissatisfied masses. With the turn of the century, the deficiencies of the period, known as Porfirismo, began to emerge like corpses thrown into a lake with the hope that they would not be trouble in the future. Mexico certainly had an incipient industry, but the mining, railroad, large-scale agriculture, and financial sectors were in foreign hands, mainly American. Resentment was rampant both among the middle classes—who received fewer wages than American workers who did the same jobs—and the peasantry. To maintain calm and peace, Díaz had eliminated the freedom of the press, political parties, unions, and anyone who opposed him by any means necessary, including exile and murder. The first death rattles of the regime began in 1906 and 1907. In those years, two strikes broke out in the mining company of Cananea and a textile company named Río Blanco. Despite the fact that the strikers, unwilling to tolerate more injustice and mistreatment by their foreign masters, begged President Díaz to intercede, the general brutally repressed the workers. In the Río Blanco factory, located in the state of Veracruz, gunshots were heard for several days as the forces of order liquidated the strikers, who fled to the hills.

Díaz, of course, was not unaware of the country's situation, the widespread fears that the United States would appropriate more territory, and the dissatisfaction with the attitude of the country's real owners. Mexico's dependence on the business cycle of the United States, as well as Theodore Roosevelt's "big stick" policy, his corollary to the Monroe Doctrine, worried President Díaz so much that in his later years, he began to approach European investors in order to shield Mexico from US annexationist ideology, which had become so strident that it had its hungry eyes on Mexico's northern states. Porfirio Díaz is credited with the phrase that sums up his concern for the neighbor to the north: "Poor Mexico, so far from God and so close to the United States!"

Throughout its history as an independent nation, Mexico had attracted the interests of the great powers due to its geographical position and natural resources. At the beginning of the 20th century, large oil fields were discovered, and Mexico became the world's third-largest producer of what is known as liquid gold. Díaz granted liberal concessions for its exploitation, which made the country even more desirable for foreign investors. Mexico's gold and silver mineral riches were legendary. And the demand for Mexican crops, such as coffee, rubber, and henequen, aroused the greed of international capitalists. As world demand increased and foreign powers expanded their economic interests around the globe, Mexico was on its way to becoming the battlefield of great global interests.

But the most immediate cause for the coming collapse of the old regime was the situation of the rural class, which made up the vast majority of the country. The peasants, chained to large plantations in the south of the country, lived in semi-slavery, suffering physical abuse, and they were indebted for life due to the haciendas, as the bosses paid in kind, never in cash. The peasants' debts were inherited from parents to children, which only perpetuated poverty and despair. American writer John Kenneth Turner, who visited a henequen hacienda in Yucatan during the Porfiriato, was horrified by what he saw.

Here and there among them I saw tired-looking women and children, sometimes little girls as young as eight or ten. Two thousand [henequen] leaves a day is the usual stint on [the hacienda of] San Antonio Yaxche. On other plantations I was told that it is sometimes as high as three thousand. "We come to work gladly," said another young Maya, "because we're starved. But before the end of the first week we want to run away. That is why they lock us up at night."

The first thing Turner saw on a henequen plantation was how a "slave" was whipped fifty times with a wet rope. "I saw no punishments worse than beating in Yucatan," he wrote. Women were forced to kneel when they were whipped.

The situation of the peasants is key to understanding the Mexican Revolution. By 1910, the year of Halley's Comet, land appropriation and the dispossession of communities at the hands of large landowners and the so-called delimitation companies had been going on for decades. A single family, the Terrazas of Chihuahua, owned seven million hectares alone. There are countries in the world that are smaller than that. Dispossessed peasants came to the planters to offer the only thing they had left: their hands and their work. In the eyes of the country's ruling class, they were a burden, an ignorant and lazy mass that were meant to be oppressed, subjugated, and exploited to death under the sun. "We were tough," admitted Díaz. "The poor are so ignorant that they have no power. We were tough sometimes to the point of being cruel. But all of this was necessary for the life and progress of the nation."

In 1907 and 1908, a sudden American recession that had begun on Wall Street reached Mexico, which, at this point, was highly dependent on the United States' economic cycle. Although the crisis was short-lived in America, the consequences were catastrophic for the Mexicans, who saw prices of consumption goods double while real wages fell to the floor.

The Creelman Interview

In 1908, on the eve of a new presidential election, the nearly eighty-year-old General Díaz gave an interview to a foreign journalist called James Creelman for an American monthly publication called *Pearson's Magazine*. The title of the interview was "Porfirio Díaz: Hero of the Americas," and the journalist did not hide his admiration toward the president. Creelman simply reflected the widespread idea of Díaz among industrialized nations:

There is not a more romantic or heroic figure in all the world, nor one more intensely watched by both the friends and foes of democracy, than the soldier-statesman whose adventurous youth pales the pages of Dumas, and whose iron rule has converted the warring, ignorant, superstitious and impoverished masses of Mexico, oppressed by centuries of Spanish cruelty and greed, into a strong, steady, peaceful, debt-paying and progressive nation.

Creelman forgot to mention that Díaz was a dictator who ferociously repressed any opposition.

But perhaps Creelman didn't mention it because the old general made a startling statement during the historic interview. "I can lay down the Presidency of Mexico without a pang of regret," Díaz said at the outset. Don Porfirio conceded that he had had enough and that he would welcome the emergence of an opposition party. When the interview came out, the text was read with astonished eyes by the Mexican political class. "I will welcome an opposition party. If it appears, I will see it as a blessing and not as an evil, and if it can develop power, not to exploit but to rule, I will stand by it, support it, advise it and forget myself in the successful inauguration of complete democratic government in the country." And it would be through this sudden fissure that Díaz opened that the person of the year of 1911 would make his entry: Francisco Ignacio Madero.

Chapter 3 – Francisco and the Spirits

"My friends, pulque is the best auxiliary of the dictatorship, because it degrades and it brutalizes the peoples and delivers them tied, by their hands and feet, to their executioners."

—Francisco I. Madero

The space of freedom that Díaz opened in the twenty-fourth year of his presidency could have been a moment of lucidity or perhaps a calculated move to defeat his strongest opponent, thus causing a flood of small political parties. The fact is the loophole was exploited by an improbable character, not by a peasant leader in arms, nor by an anarchist worker leader or a communist intellectual. Rather, it was by the son of one of the richest families in the country, Francisco I. Madero.

Francisco Madero was a petite man with an ample forehead, a goatee, and thick eyebrows. He was 1.57 meters tall (around 5'1") and had a deep look with eyes full of serenity. He always seemed to be a little distracted, and he suffered from a constant trembling in his left shoulder. He had studied in Paris, where he found the works of Allan Kardec, the father of Spiritism, and became interested in Spiritism himself. When he went back to Mexico, he began to practice automatic writing as a medium. The Ouija board told him that one day he would be Mexico's president. Despite being a member of one of the richest families, Madero had great social awareness. In his haciendas, he talked to his workers, learned their names, and introduced novel farming techniques that increased the land's productivity. He practiced a rigid body discipline, which meant no alcohol, no tobacco, and no meat, and he encouraged his workers to avoid alcoholism. "My friends," he said to them, "pulque is the dictatorship's best ally, because it degrades and brutalizes the people and delivers them tied, by their hands and feet, to their executioners." Filled with humanistic and philanthropic sentiments, Panchito (a nickname Francisco had, which was a loving reference to his short height) increased the wages of his workers, provided them with medical care, and introduced education to his estates, turning them into productive model units.

Considered as the black sheep of the family, all of whom had good relations with the regime and little desire to get into trouble with the government, Francisco Madero began his career as a writer in two very different genres: as a spiritualist with the nom de plume of BHIMA, and for mundane and more temporal affairs with his birth name. He took his activity as a medium very seriously; he was convinced that he could communicate with a younger brother of his who had died as a child, as well as with another deceased member of his family named José, who told Francisco that he would have to further practice self-discipline because he was going to be entrusted with a mission for the good of the country. Francisco retired to the solitude of the fields, where he fasted and went into a trance, while his father and brothers scratched their heads and thought he had gone crazy. But Madero was sure of his mission, and to him, the Díaz-Creelman interview was like an epiphany.

"A great burden weighs on your shoulders," the spirit of his brother José told Francisco in June 1908, according to the surviving journals written by Madero himself. "You have accepted a momentous mission. This year is going to become the base of your political career, since the book that you are going to write will be the standard that your citizens should judge you with; it will be the measure that will delineate you full-length, the one that reveals to the Union who you are, what your ideals, your aspirations, your aptitudes and your means of combat are." In 1909, Madero finally published his gospel, a book called *The Presidential Succession of 1910.* In its pages, he criticized the concentration of power in one man, absolutism, and the lack of democracy. He criticized the consequences of land dispossession and its concentration in the hands of the few, as well as the alcoholism among farmworkers, illiteracy, and the repression of the nonconformists, but Madero dared not criticize the system itself. His book established the need for a legal-political framework that guaranteed freedom for the citizens and stated that this framework should be respected by the president. It was, in this sense, a cautious and conservative book—it did not talk about revolutions. Madero also took care not to attack Díaz personally; he only wondered what would happen after his death, which everyone was expecting, if the roads to democracy were not opened.

"Dear brother," his beloved spirits disclosed to Madero in his journal entry corresponding to October 27th, 1908, "you cannot imagine the effect that your book will produce in the Republic, especially when the electoral work begins in Coahuila, and take them [sic] to the capital for the organization of the democratic party, which should be accelerated as much as possible, once the electoral campaign begins." The spirits were not mistaken. The book caused a sensation among the political and intellectual elite. Madero's anti-reelection party nominated him to run for the presidency in the 1910 elections against General Porfirio Díaz, who was beginning to dislike that small annoyance of northern Mexico.

1910, the year of the elections, arrived. Madero made a genuine electoral campaign throughout the country, perhaps the first all-out campaign in Mexico's history. He visited several cities where he was already famous. One or two places received him coldly, but he usually gathered crowds. In Guadalajara and Monterrey, the largest cities in Mexico after the capital, more than 10,000 people went to cheer him on, which was an outrageous number, at least for Díaz. Nobody had seen such free-wheeling gatherings in support of anyone other than the president. In Mexico City, Madero gathered 50,000 people electrified by his proposal of effective suffrage and no reelection.

The persecution against Francisco started to materialize through minor issues—a small penalty in money and an investigation for an alleged fraud he never committed in the purchase of livestock—and the hostile tide was growing. Fearing for his safety, Francisco's grandfather wrote a letter to President Díaz, asking him to be lenient with his grandson since he had something wrong with his head, as Francisco believed that supernatural beings were guiding him.

In this caustic letter, Evaristo Madero told Díaz: "No one like you can understand, my distinguished friend, from the experience you have, and the long years you have lived, that in a large family it is common for some member to have extravagant ideas." Díaz did not flinch because he had everything under control. The expected elections were held in June. The day was tense, and if Madero had had hopes of achieving democratic change, his dreams were crushed when he was arrested shortly before election day. He was isolated, and no one could see him, even though hundreds of his followers came to the prison to protest on the day of his arrest. On August 21st, the overwhelming triumph of Porfirio Díaz was announced, as he had carried the election with 98 percent of the vote. According to the electoral results, Madero had only obtained 2 percent of the votes.

Positively certain that the hornet's nest that had been stirred up had passed, President Díaz decided to free Madero at the pleas of his family, who reiterated that he was the weird son and that they had never supported his foray into politics. Francisco boarded a train north but did not stop at home. He continued to the United States, where he had friends. He established himself in the city of Saint Louis and, after deep meditation, wrote a plan called the Plan of San

Luis de Potosí, named after the city where he had been incarcerated in a diminutive prison cell.

According to the plan, he effectively assumed the provisional presidency of Mexico and called on the country to take up arms on November 20th, a Sunday. Madero, a pacifist, declared the 1910 elections illegal and called for violence, and he summoned the people to rise around him because he saw no other way. It was a bold move, considering that there had been no triumphant rebellion in Mexico for decades. The plan also demanded free and democratic elections, and Madero also mentioned the issue of land dispossession by the haciendas, which would have to offer restitution of some kind. "The time has come," he wrote in prison.

November 20th was also the Feast of Christ the King, the holiday that marks the end of the Catholic liturgical calendar and thus the end of a cycle— a date with apocalyptic overtones, although it is not known if Madero chose that date with metaphysics in his mind. In one of the last communications Madero had with his brother's spirit, he was told, "Your destiny is great; you have a very important mission to fulfill. It is necessary that in all your deeds you are up to the task. An enormous responsibility weighs on you. You have seen, thanks to the spiritual illumination that you receive from us, the abyss where your country is precipitating. You would be a coward if you don't prevent it. You have also seen the path that the country must follow to save itself. Woe to you if by your weakness, your faintness, your lack of energy, you do not guide it courageously along that path." Madero distributed the plan by mail, sent people to speed the insurrection, appointed provisional governors of the states, and asked the people to respond to his call. The die was cast.

Chapter 4 – Victory Comes Too Soon

"Nothing ever happens in Mexico until it happens."

—Porfirio Díaz

November 20th, 1910, arrived. At one point, Francisco considered abandoning everything and boarding a steamer to Argentina, but his spirits—or perhaps his inner voice—did not fail him. On the appointed day, there were uprisings in several parts of Mexico. Such was the impact of the events that, in a country where everything was repressed effectively and silently, the newspapers in the capital were talking about "the seditious" on the front page two days later. There were clashes with the federal forces and destruction of some bridges and telegraph lines here and there. The press also printed false news that Madero had been captured, all to give some assurance of the stability of the government to the citizens, who were rushing to the magazine stands to buy the papers. A week later, the *New York American* published a telegram from General Díaz, who was trying to calm things down. He said that the Mexican people loved peace and would not accept a revolution, that foreigners had nothing to fear, and that there had only been a few riots in four states: Puebla, Durango, Chihuahua, and Tamaulipas.

But Díaz had miscalculated terribly. Mexico was ripe for a revolution. In the northern states, where there was a tradition of independence and rejection of the central government, and where people had easier access to arms via the United States, there was a real popular uprising. The rebellion in Chihuahua was the first to seriously worry the old dictator. One of the rebel leaders was a former bandit who had changed his name and was now going by the moniker of "Pancho Villa." He later said he had changed his name because he killed a federal soldier who had raped his sister.

At the same time, Emiliano Zapata rose in the south. He was similar in many ways and yet different from Villa. Zapata, a tall, tanned, good-looking peasant with deep eyes and a stern expression, gathered a rural army from the plantations and villages of southern Mexico, seized the lands of the haciendas, and began distributing them among the peasants of Anenecuilco, his hometown. Meanwhile, Francisco Madero was still in the United States, following the news with enthusiasm. He tried to cross into Mexico to lead the rebellion, but after a disastrous episode in which he himself tried to lead some rebels to battle, he returned to the United States, waiting for a better occasion to appear.

"Now we can exert a great influence on him," the spirits dictated to Francisco, referring to President Díaz, "because he no longer has his old vigor and his energy has decreased considerably, while the powerful passions that moved him have diminished with the years." But the revolutionaries in northern Mexico were not interested in metaphysical realities, only in earthly ones. The popular armies were made up of workers who could not find employment in the mines, landless peasants, manual workers tired of the mistreatment at the haciendas, small farm owners threatened by large landowners, and hostile cowboys who had lost their freedom of movement. In 1911, the rebels attacked the strategic Ciudad Juárez along the US border, right at the place where the Rio Grande makes a turn north. Across the river was the city of El Paso, Texas.

The revolutionary forces numbered 3,500 men, while the government's defenders were only 675 stunned soldiers who had never expected an uprising of that magnitude. Madero showed his good-natured and pacifist personality for the first time in Ciudad Juárez. He sent a letter to the general defending the plaza, inviting him to suspend hostilities so as not to get into trouble with the United States. The general agreed, but the revolutionary troops under the command of Pancho Villa and Pascual Orozco continued the attack.

There are photographs of Americans watching the Battle of Ciudad Juárez from El Paso. Some are perched on train wagons with spy glasses. A postcard showing a dozen businessmen-looking spectators watching the Battle of Ciudad Juárez reads: "On the roof garden of Hotel Paso del Norte, the only hotel in the world offering its guests a safe, comfortable place to view a Mexican revolution." However, the free show was not as safe as the postcard boasted. Some lost bullets flew into the other country, and the United States complained to Mexican authorities that there were a few wounded citizens.

Illustration 1. American tourists in El Paso gather atop the Hotel Paso del Norte. Unknown photographer, 1911. Collection of Colonel Henry G. Moseley, USA.

Revolutionary troops cornered the federal army in downtown Juárez and finally seized the famous city of Paso del Norte. Villa and

Orozco went after the enemy leaders who had been captured to shoot them, but Francisco Madero, the compassionate revolutionary, intervened. Before Villa reached the prisoners, Madero helped General Juan Navarro and his officers escape to the United States in order to save their lives. He took them to the border in his own car and crossed the Rio Grande. The incident sparked bitter disagreement between the rebel leaders and the intellectual father of the revolution, but the troops were loyal to Madero, and Villa and Orozco ceased for the time being. The incident was, however, a preview of the dilemmas Madero was about to face.

The *Ypiranga*

The press was loyal to the government, and they described the revolutionaries as dangerous bandits and reported that the situation was under control, but Díaz knew better. The country was on fire, from the north to the south.

At the other end of the country, 12,000 peasants joined Zapata, who seized the haciendas, distributed the land among his peasants, and refused the usual bribes. "Check the colonial titles and take what belongs legitimately to the people." His scope was eminently local. When asked by the authorities whether he was an ally of Madero's— that is, if he had joined the revolution—he simply said he was returning the land to its rightful owners, the ancestral communities of Mexico. Zapata captured his first important city, Cuautla, after a long siege that came to an end when his men poured gasoline in the city's aqueduct, thus creating a curtain of fire that cut through the town.

President Díaz sent his friends to negotiate with the rebels while at the same time sending a bill to Congress prohibiting reelection. He also made Cabinet changes and expanded the military's budget to dominate the rebellion. The "Strong Man of the Americas" only gave up when the president of the United States, William H. Taft, deployed 20,000 soldiers to the border and dispatched several navy ships to the most important Mexican ports. It is possible that by this point, Madero had the support of the United States, and Taft no longer considered Díaz as someone who could guarantee the interests of the US. Díaz's most important minister, Finance Minister José Yves Limantour, spoke frankly with Díaz: "If the internal war continues, the United States will intervene." That day, the old man understood that his days at the National Palace were finally over.

On the night of May 21ˢᵗ, 1911, under the light of a car's headlights, the Treaty of Ciudad Juárez was signed in front of the closed customs, pursuant to which Díaz and the vice president would resign their posts. Secretary of Foreign Relations Francisco León de la Barra would assume the provisional presidency and call for elections, and the revolutionaries would cease hostilities. On May 25ᵗʰ, the dictator resigned before Congress. In his farewell address, he said that the people had showered him with honors, that a group of "millenarian gangs" had rebelled against him, that he did not know of any reason attributable to him that motivated that social event, and that he was resigning in order to avoid further bloodshed. In his grandiloquent style, he claimed, "I hope, gentlemen, that once the passions have subsided, a more thorough assessment will give rise to a correct judgment that will allow me to die bearing, in the depths of my soul, a fair correlation with the affection that I have given to my compatriots all my life." When the speech ended, the deputies applauded loudly and threw cheers for General Díaz. The next day, Francisco León de la Barra, one of Díaz's trusted men, took possession. It wasn't a very revolutionary transition, but Madero had achieved what he wanted.

Ten days after the Treaty of Ciudad Juárez, Díaz took a last walk through the city of Veracruz, located on the Gulf coast, and boarded the *Ypiranga,* a German-registered passenger and cargo steamer, which would take him to Spain. Escorted by the port's military commander, and standing next to his wife, Díaz received an ovation on his walk to the ship, while a dozen pretty young girls threw bunches of roses before the now-retired president. Some of them stepped forward to present the flowers personally. The cream of society went up to Díaz's cabins to say goodbye to the family, and a band played the Mexican national anthem. A middle-aged general with white hair and a gray mustache called Victoriano Huerta hugged Díaz warmly and said that he could always count on the army. Díaz's last words to those left on the pier were, "I shall die in Mexico."

Unaware of these demonstrations of loyalty to Don Porfirio, Madero traveled south to make his epoch-making entrance at the capital as the leader of the triumphant revolution. Early on the morning of June 7th, 1911, the day scheduled to receive Madero, there was an earthquake in Mexico City, where more than fifty people lost their lives. A few hours later, another earthquake was experienced, this time a civil one, for in the midst of extraordinary popular joy, which had not been seen in a long time, Madero entered Mexico City. He was welcomed as a hero. Geologically and politically, the capital of the republic was shaken to its foundations.

In their desire to see the man who had commanded the most far-reaching movement ever to change the political conditions in Mexico, people formed in solid masses along the railroad, from the suburbs to the colonial station of the national railway. They filled the huge train shed and yards, and they packed both sides of the streets leading from the station to the national palace, a distance of more than a mile. It was with great difficulty that the lines of soldiers were able to preserve a lane down the broad Paseo de la Reforma for the passage of the automobiles that carried the guests. From the time Madero left the patio of the train station to enter the waiting coach, there was not a moment that was not punctuated with cheers. Francisco's dream had been accomplished: he had overthrown Díaz and organized new elections in which he would be the presidential candidate. Naturally.

It had been the "perfect revolution," efficient and with hardly any bloodshed. It had been no more than half a year since November 20th. If the ghosts said something to Francisco in those days, we do not know it because he did not leave a record. But his rival, Díaz, who was much more experienced when it came to the Mexicans, had left with a warning for the compassionate revolutionary: "Madero has unleashed a tiger. Now let us see if he can control it."

President Madero

On May 25th, 1911, a character with smooth manners and the looks of an aristocrat named Francisco León de la Barra, who had served as the secretary of foreign relations in the last years of the Porfiriato, took office as the provisional president. One of his great achievements as foreign minister had been the organization of the first binational meeting between the presidents of Mexico and the United States, Porfirio Díaz and William Taft, in the city of El Paso. The summit had almost ended in tragedy, as the police arrested a man with a gun who had been approaching the podium. He was caught only a few steps away from both presidents, and who knows how history would have unfolded had he succeeded in killing both heads of state. Luckily for Foreign Minister León de la Barra, the meeting ended without incident.

Throughout its history, the Foreign Office has been one of the most important posts in Mexico, as the man responsible for the position had to perform balancing acts between the great powers of the world and deal with its mighty neighbor, the United States. That Díaz chose his foreign secretary as his successor says a lot about what the old soldier considered to be the most important issue in Mexico in the 1910s: foreign policy. In the face of an unstable country, foreign powers were lurking like birds of prey over Mexico's natural resources.

De la Barra, a member of one of the country's wealthiest families, had a long diplomatic career, although he had no political experience. He had met Queen Isabella II of Spain, called "the woman with the sad destiny," and he represented Mexico on the four-hundredth anniversary of the discovery of the Americas. At his inauguration, de la Barra gave a succinct speech. He claimed that his main objective was to reestablish peace, that under no circumstances would he accept being a candidate for the presidency in the new elections that he would oversee, and that he would guarantee the fairness of the democratic process. Francisco Madero congratulated him on his position, and the new president, in turn, congratulated the leader of the revolution for "his patriotic and dignified attitude" in creating a new era of peace and progress. De la Barra also mentioned that the revolutionary troops would have to surrender their weapons and demobilize. Madero began relaying messages to his troops that they should present themselves at the agreed points and hand over their pistols, rifles, and machetes since the federal army was the only legitimate force in Mexico. In southern and northern Mexico, Zapata and Villa must have removed their hats to scratch their disheveled heads. Villa possibly laughed, as he knew better. Zapata must have frowned. Was *that* a revolution?

As the candidate for the presidency for four political parties, Madero presented as his platform on the principle of "No reelection" and promised to carry out reforms to regulate the political party system and the elections, convert the judicial system, strengthen small rural properties, establish equitable taxes, abolish the death penalty, respect the freedom of the press, promote public education, maintain the separation of church and state, and deploy a conciliatory policy to rebuild the country's economy. Not bad, but for the revolutionary peasants in arms, unemployed workers, and impoverished families, it was like applying new paint to a house in ruins. On the other hand, Madero's program was not something that disturbed the establishment; actually, they were all reforms that many of them had been expecting for years. Furthermore, to the satisfaction of the upper class, Francisco, who detested violence and bloodbath, was pressuring his old allies to disarm as soon as possible, those very men who had taken him to the highest position in the nation. And they were not pleased.

When the elections were held, there was only one name in the mind of the country: Madero. Francisco won the presidency with 99.26 percent of the vote. For Mexicans, the short man with the gentle expression and goatee was the David that had faced Goliath and then defeated him. It was an unthinkable feat. The transmission of power was carried out in the Ambassadors Room before the diplomatic representatives of the nations with which Mexico had relations. The ministers of Belgium, China, Norway, Germany, Austria, Hungary, Chile, Japan, Brazil, Britain, Spain, and the United States were all present, among others. The United States ambassador, Henry Lane Wilson, talked to the president on behalf of the diplomatic corps. A day before the ceremony, Madero promised the American correspondent for *New York World* that in three months, there would be complete peace in the country. Then he went out to greet the people on the esplanade. With Madero in power, and Díaz far away on the other side of the Atlantic, spending his last years as a tourist, the revolution had smoothly come to an end. Cabinet members embraced and congratulated each other. There were hugs, patriotic music, and chants of "*Viva!*" Few imagined that the storm had barely started.

Chapter 5 – The Wicked Ambassador

"When Madero first attracted my attention, he was engaged in the business of making incendiary speeches, usually of very little intellectual merit,

before audiences in remote parts of Mexico."

—Henry Lane Wilson, US Ambassador to Mexico

The honeymoon between Madero and the Mexicans did not last. From the outset, he had many fires to extinguish and few hands to do it. Pascual Orozco, one of the northern rebels who had responded to his call in the Plan of San Luis, rebelled in Chihuahua. Despite the fact that Orozco was one of his old supporters, Madero had no choice but to send the army to fight him. Meanwhile, the press mocked him. Knowing his fondness for Spiritism, newspapers called the president the "madman who communicates with the dead." This heckling, though, was the result of the freedom of the press that he himself had established. In the south, Emiliano Zapata and his peasants were desperate, seeing how slowly the one change that interested them most was being approached. This change wasn't the freedom of the press, democracy, peace, or the separation of church and state; all of these were concerns of the intellectuals. His creed and faith made him believe in recovering the communal lands: *Tierra y Libertad,* "Land and Freedom." Madero insisted that he had to observe legal procedures. When Zapata finally got to know Madero in Mexico City, he suffered a great disappointment.

President Madero had heard rumors that Zapata's army was made of "barbarians," but he had also expressed his sincere appreciation for the southern leader's contribution to the triumph of the revolution. Madero received him at his house in Mexico City, and when he asked him about the number of troops under his command, the polite and nervous president told Zapata that he would no longer need his services and that the peasants should surrender their weapons since the revolution had triumphed. Zapata burned with indignation. Trying to remain calm, he said that he didn't trust the old federal Porfirian army, which was still in place and untouched, and he warned the president that they would not surrender until he returned the lands to the peasants.

"No, General," Madero replied. "The time for the weapons has passed; now the fight is going to take place in a different field. The Revolution needs to guarantee order, to be respectful of property." Zapata, sullen and not given to diplomacy, stood up without letting go of the rifle he was carrying, which, according to eyewitnesses, he kept next to his body even during the meal. Zapata nodded toward the gold chain watch that Madero was wearing and asked him, "Look, Mr. Madero: if I, taking advantage of the fact that I am carrying a gun, take your golden watch and keep it to myself, and after a while we meet each other, both armed and with an equal force, would you have the right to demand me to return it to you?" Madero seemed surprised at the question. "Of course, General, and I would even have the right to ask you for compensation for the time you misused it!" he said. Zapata took a step forward. "That's exactly what happened to us in the state of Morelos. A few hacienda owners seized the lands of the communities. My soldiers, the armed peasants and the people sent me to tell you, with all due respect, that the restitution of their lands should be carried out immediately."

Francisco was worried because he knew that Orozco's and Zapata's anger was just, but he had first promised to restore peace. The rebellions in the north and south contributed to the erosion of the presidential authority, but Madero's greatest menace was a sinister character who acted as a lawyer for the big oil companies and, incidentally, was the ambassador of the United States, Henry Lane Wilson. Wilson looked like a cowboy. He was tall and thin and wore an outdated haircut, parted in the middle. He had enormous power because he was the only ambassador in Mexico— the other countries had only "representatives" or envoys—and because of this, he had a great influence on the diplomatic corps. However, his greatest leverage was that he could decide when the United States should intervene militarily in Mexico. On his recommendation, the US Army and Navy could mobilize immediately. Or at least that's what he boasted.

Wilson never hid his dislike for Madero and his longing for the old regime. On one occasion, Wilson referred to Porfirio Díaz's "wisdom, sobriety and patriotism" after he was gone. Wilson saw Mexico as a country in chaos and believed that Madero had opened Pandora's box and was unable to control it. When Ambassador Wilson learned that Pancho Villa had attacked American property in northern Mexico, he threatened Madero with intervention by the United States. Madero responded indignantly that this would be a declaration of war, but the ambassador did not blink. Madero sent General Victoriano Huerta to control Villa. Huerta, the old general who had hugged Díaz on board the *Ypiranga* steamer and had promised him the army's loyalty, hated Villa. As soon as he had him in his hands, he took the first occasion to arrest him and have him shot. Villa was sent blindfolded against an adobe wall and heard the sound of the guns aiming at him. At the last moment, though, Madero's family stepped in. They convinced Huerta to send him to prison in Mexico City instead. Now, Madero was at odds with those who had been his greatest supporters, with the ambassador of the United States, with his own generals, and with the press, which continued to fiercely attack him. With the strikes, rebellions, peasant protests, and the anarchy that everyone thought they saw, observers increasingly came to the idea that Madero could not guarantee stability. Wilson, who represented the interests of the United States, went berserk when Madero ordered that all railroad employees that worked for the Americans must speak Spanish. The ambassador protested so vehemently that he forced Madero to rescind the order.

The worst part was that Madero's presence no longer aroused the same enthusiasm among the middle class because they thought he was being weak with Zapata, infirm with Villa, hesitant with the other rebels, and did not make them go silent with a bullet, as Díaz had done, but negotiated with them. The press called him "the midget Madero" and printed cruel cartoons that mocked his short stature and suggested his diminished masculinity. Finally, in October 1912, Félix Díaz rebelled in Veracruz. Félix had a familiar name to the ears of the people—he was the nephew of President Porfirio Díaz, and the Mexican aristocracy, with Ambassador Wilson leading the ovation, applauded the news, thinking that the old order was going to be restored. He was, after all, Don Porfirio's own blood and a military man as well. Wilson was pleased with what he saw as an imminent change of power favorable to the US.

But the ambassador had calculated badly. Félix Díaz was defeated and sentenced to death. Again, the humanist Madero changed the death penalty to life imprisonment. With this order, he sealed his luck. This time, more implacable and ruthless forces than those he had fought in 1910 were about to engulf him completely.

The Ten Tragic Days

The furious backlash came in February 1913. In the north, concession-owning foreigners were financing rebels like Pascual Orozco, and everywhere, the federal army was resentful. Madero did not yet believe that his generals could plot against him, but at dawn on February 9th, 1913, one of the most brutal and deplorable incidents of the Mexican Revolution and of Mexican history began, an episode known as *La Decena Trágica*, or the Ten Tragic Days, when downtown Mexico City became a battlefield.

It all began when the disgruntled generals revolted, released General Félix Díaz from prison, and organized a coup to depose Madero. The insurrectionists marched to the National Palace, the seat of the presidential power in Mexico—the equivalent of the White House in the United States—and seized the building. Madero was sleeping in Chapultepec Castle, a mile from the capital. They woke up the president early in the morning to inform him that there was a revolt in Mexico City. Francisco knew that he had to make an appearance in the capital to demonstrate that the situation was under control, but he had few troops at his disposal. The military college was in the castle, so he called the young students to escort him along the Paseo de la Reforma avenue to the main square.

Escorted by 300 cadets, who were dressed in their gala uniforms, several members of the Cabinet, and a few friends, Madero took off from the castle toward the National Palace. He rode his horse along Paseo de la Reforma, holding a Mexican flag, among the applause of the astonished people who saw him. More people joined the column, although, at some point, they had to stop due to bullets flying at them, the source of which remains unknown. That moment is remembered in Mexico every February 9th as the March of Loyalty. A series of photographs taken that day by Gerónimo Hernández, who was running alongside the president, shows him on an imposing horse, waving Mexico's flag as he headed to the main square. Francisco is smiling, greeting the people with his hat. He is followed by groups of people who change with each photograph. Besides his ministers, wearing dark suits, ties, and hats, there are peasants, men in overalls, and youths with suspenders, working clothes, and old-fashioned berets. In several photos, an anonymous boy walks in front of the horse, turning his head to look at Madero. In one of the narrow streets downtown, a disheveled man greets the president with a mashed beret who has already seen its best days. Francisco still salutes with his hat.

Illustration 2. Madero during the March of Loyalty.
Photo by Gerónimo Hernández 1913.
Fondo Casasola, INAH, Mexico.

Moments earlier, a loyal general had recovered the National Palace, but behind them came a larger contingent led by rebel general Bernardo Reyes. Both forces clashed in the main square. Pro-Madero general Lauro Villar Ochoa demanded Reyes three times to surrender. The civilian population looked at the scene incredulously, thinking that they would be safe. Reyes threw his horse against Villar to crush him, and at that moment, the fight with machine guns began. Bernardo Reyes fell, pierced, and so did many of the civilians who were watching. The rebels escaped to a fortress and arms warehouse known as *La Ciudadela*, the Citadel, which aggravated the situation instead of making it better, since 27 guns, 8,500 rifles, 100 machine guns, 5,000 howitzers, and twenty million cartridges were stored there and were now at their disposal. Mexico City was about to become a battlefield. When Madero arrived with his contingent at the National Palace, he saw dozens of dead bodies. Many of them were people who had gone to the morning mass.

Ten days of fighting followed. The extra edition of that afternoon's newspaper described the city as a "river of blood." On the first day alone, more than 800 people were killed, most of them civilians. At the headquarters of the presidential seat, Madero put Victoriano Huerta in charge of the defense. Madero's brother warned him that Huerta was going to betray him. Francisco summoned Huerta and questioned him. After seeing what he thought was loyalty in his eyes, Francisco ratified Huerta as a defender of the city. On February 11th, Huerta attacked the Citadel, where the rebels were hiding. But Huerta put his own men directly in the line of fire of the machine guns, and the streets were littered with corpses. It was not a mistake or simply a blunder on Huerta's part; he had made this decision on purpose. The white-haired general, who had hugged Porfirio Díaz on the steamer and had met with his nephew Félix, had secretly allied with the coup leaders. Together, they had agreed to get rid of Madero. While the plotters destroyed the city with grenades to create a terrifying effect and provoke international alarm, Huerta sent his own troops to unknowingly commit suicide in areas previously established with Félix Díaz. No one in the National Palace understood why the besieged resisted, especially since the reinforcements had reached the city.

Each house became a fortress. The women ran from one side of the street to the other to search for food, carrying white sheets like truce flags as they zigzagged between piles of corpses. The United States embassy car rushed by with an American flag, trying to avoid the bullets. Many photographers risked their lives in capturing the events, but thanks to them, we can see exactly what happened in the heart of the city. Hundreds of photos document the level of destruction in the capital: families piled up in the safest room of the house waiting for the bombardment, mountains of corpses cremated in the fields of Balbuena to avoid an epidemic, and women offering the soldiers a drink of water through their windows.

Meanwhile, a friend of the conspirators met with the alarmed diplomatic corps: the United States ambassador, Henry Lane Wilson. At the beginning of the Ten Tragic Days, Wilson had visited Madero to protest against the savagery of the war, and he threatened him with a military intervention in order to protect the foreign residents. As the self-appointed leader of the diplomatic corps, Henry Lane Wilson told the foreign diplomats that they should ask for Madero's resignation, an action that was clearly out of line.

On the sixth day, the ambassador met with the secretary of foreign relations, Pedro Lascuráin, and told him that he had the power to deploy 3,000 to 4,000 US soldiers to Mexico if order was not restored and that the only way to restore the law was if Madero resigned. From that meeting, he returned to the diplomatic corps to report on his conversation with Lascuráin, although he admitted that, with respect to the American troops, he had been boasting. He immediately sent Spain's minister to ask Madero for his resignation. Indignant, Francisco screamed that they had no right to ask him for such a thing and threw him out.

The next step for the US ambassador was to try to convince the Senate—where Porfirio Díaz still had supporters and friends—to ask for Madero's resignation. A group of them agreed to go and talk to the president, while Wilson sent cables to the United States speaking against Madero and in favor of the rebels in the Citadel. He was in a hurry. President Taft had less than one month left in office, and there was a president-elect—Thomas Woodrow Wilson—who sympathized with Madero. It was a well-orchestrated conspiracy, with flyers against the president being printed in the basement of the United States Embassy. As the days progressed, Henry Lane Wilson invited Victoriano Huerta and Félix Díaz to the embassy to decide who would be the new president. They even appointed a Cabinet.

On the last night, Huerta invited Gustavo Madero, Francisco's brother, to have dinner with him. After dinner, he took him to the Citadel, where Gustavo was lynched by the insurrectionists, who plucked his glass eye with the point of their bayonets and began playing with it, throwing it to one another like a ball. Then they mutilated him. Francisco and the vice president were arrested by a general loyal to Huerta and then locked in a room in the National Palace. Huerta asked Henry Lane Wilson what he should do with Madero. "You decide, I hope you send him to a madhouse!" was his answer. So, Huerta assumed he had the go-ahead from the US to do whatever he wanted with the president. Francisco's parents, sisters, and wife Sara applied for asylum at the Japanese Embassy. The Cuban envoy, fearing for the lives of the president and vice president, offered them political asylum, but Huerta had other plans. Francisco's wife, Sara, ventured outside the Japanese Embassy to beg Ambassador Wilson to intercede for his husband. Wilson, from his arrogant heights, replied laconically that he had warned Francisco that this would happen and that her husband was simply paying the consequences for his bad government.

At ten o'clock on the night of February 22nd, while Madero tried to sleep but instead laid in bed, curled up and crying because his mother had informed him that his brother Gustavo had been brutally tortured and murdered, a door opened. A group of soldiers came in and informed the president and vice president that they would be transferred to a prison while their relocation to Cuba was arranged. As they approached the prison, the car transporting Madero kept going and headed for the plains behind the building. The automobile stopped, and the men ordered Francisco to get out of the vehicle. There was a burning flash on the nape of his neck. Under the starry sky, "Maderito," as his friend Pancho Villa used to call him, fell dead on the grass. A warm pool of blood formed under his battered head.

Chapter 6 – Victoriano Huerta

"Honest and decent people don't come near me,
   so I have to govern with the scoundrels."
—Victoriano Huerta

Pancho Villa heard about Madero's murder while in Texas. Shortly before the Tragic Ten Days, he had escaped from prison in Mexico City disguised as a lawyer. He took the train north to seek refuge in El Paso, where he stayed in a hotel under his real name, Doroteo Arango. He kept carrier pigeons in his room to communicate with his allies in Chihuahua, located in northern Mexico. He had returned to civilian life, riding his motorcycle through the streets of El Paso, and in the afternoons, he sat at a bar where he spoke with other exiled Mexicans. Sometimes he would pay a visit to the Elite Confectionery, a store where he would buy ice cream and strawberry sodas. He was an anonymous Mexican in Texas for the time being, but the latest events, the murder of his friend "Maderito," whom he had loved and respected, aroused his fury.

In Mexico City, Ambassador Wilson and Victoriano Huerta—about whom the best thing people could whisper behind his back was that he was a drunkard—tried to give the coup d'état a legal appearance. Before murdering Madero, they forced him to sign his resignation while at the same time promising to respect his life and his family and send them to exile in Cuba. Presidential power passed, by law, to the secretary of foreign relations, Pedro Lascuráin. As president of Mexico, Lascuráin achieved a banal Guinness World Record, which is the only thing he is now remembered for: he had the shortest presidency on record, somewhere between 15 to 45 minutes, depending on the source. It was a symptom of the times. In his brief tenure as president, all he did was appoint Victoriano Huerta as the secretary of the interior and then resign. Thus, automatically, Huerta, the general with the gray mustache, a coat full of medals, and the eternal scowl, became the new strong man. In the Metropolitan Cathedral of Mexico City, the bishop offered a *Te Deum* (a short religious service of thanks), and the well-to-do breathed a sigh of relief.

The humble people went on Monday morning to the place where Madero's body had fallen to place stones and make small mounds, a Mexican custom. Others brought branches and flowers. When the coffin with the corpse left the prison, the crowd erupted in "wild screams," according to a newspaper of the time that had no qualms about calling them "people of the lowest social class" and stating that they deserved punishment for such a scandal. From there, Francisco's body was taken to La Piedad Cemetery. More than 2,000 people followed the coffin, screaming proclamations or crying openly. The police had to disperse the crowd. As Easter approached in 1913, people began to murmur that Madero was going to resurrect. His grave looked like a garden because people kept placing flowers and plants on it. Like another king had done nineteen centuries before with another tomb, Huerta ordered guards to be placed on the grave because he feared that the corpse would be stolen on Easter Sunday and that the superstitious would drag the people behind them.

Thanks to the guards, Holy Week passed without incident in Mexico City. But if Huerta had hoped that having Madero six feet underground would put an end to his troubles, he was terribly wrong.

The Astronomer

In his youth, Victoriano Huerta had been one of the best mathematicians and astronomers in Mexico. From a very poor family of indigenous origin, the young José Victoriano had entered the prestigious Heroic Military College on the recommendation of President Benito Juárez, a national hero. There, Huerta proved himself to be one of the best students. At the head of several cartographic expeditions, he made maps of the southern part of the country and had almost gone on an expedition to Japan to observe the transit of Venus in 1874. As a young cadet, Huerta lost the opportunity to study military science in Germany because he preferred to stay home to take care of his sick mother. Instead of meeting the Kaiser, he went to fight other Native Americans like him in Yucatan, where the Mayan Caste War was sweeping the peninsula. Military life in Mexico had hardened him. Huerta was reputed to have committed massacres against the Native Americans, was feared for his cruelty but recognized for his dedication and loyalty to his superiors (which had convinced Madero that he could be trusted), and was a heavy drinker. His adversaries made jokes about his constant drunkenness. By the time he became president, his vice had reached alarming levels.

Some saw in Huerta a tough and cruel person, but others saw a strong man, a replica of Don Porfirio. To those people, Huerta was someone who could guarantee peace in a country that was coming apart like a house in flames and shattering international confidence in Mexico, with the consequent drop in the share prices of large companies. On the other hand, with a president like Victoriano Huerta, the promise of real change could be ruled out. The poverty of the working classes, the dispossession of land, the semi-slavery on the haciendas, and the hunger of most of the country's population remained painful realities. For now, Huerta found the national treasury empty, and there wasn't much he could do. He wanted to rebuild the country's infrastructure, and he tried to get loans from abroad, especially from France and Great Britain.

In the United States, Woodrow Wilson took office in March 1914, and in regards to Mexico, he demonstrated that he was not sympathetic to Huerta. In his opinion, he was a usurper. When President Wilson learned from an investigating commission what his ambassador in Mexico had done during the Ten Tragic Days, he was shocked and immediately removed him from his post. Certainly, his antipathy toward Huerta was also fueled by the fact that the Mexican president was in deals with Europe, specifically with a hostile Germany.

President Wilson pressured France and Britain not to grant credits to Mexico. Germany did not abandon Huerta, in part because it was doing the same thing it had done in several peripheral countries: financing movements hostile to its enemies in the face of the impending global conflagration. The German ambassador had offered ammunition and weapons to Mexico on the condition that it stop selling oil to Britain in the event of war. Huerta agreed. In 1914, the *Ypiranga* steamer—the same German ship that had taken Porfirio Díaz to exile—left Germany for the port of Veracruz with a large shipment of weapons for the man with the perpetual scowl.

The American Invasion

In April 1914, the United States sent warships to the Gulf of Mexico to capture the city of Veracruz, the most important port in Mexico. At the head of the expedition was Admiral Frank Fletcher. His orders were to seize the customs of Veracruz and prevent the weapons from entering the country. At eleven o'clock in the morning, 800 Marines made headway to the port in boats. Defending the city was an old general called Gustavo Maass.

A few minutes before, a soldier had approached Maas to tell him that he had a call from the United States Consulate. He took the phone. The secretary of the US Consulate informed him, on behalf of the United States consul, that Admiral Frank Fletcher had orders to disembark and take the port and that Fletcher hoped there would be no resistance and bloodshed could be avoided. The minor-league bureaucrat added that General Maass should remain in his barracks and take no action when Fletcher took the trains and rolling stock at the station.

Maass barked that he could not consent to the landing and that, with the elements at his disposal, he would repel any aggression against national sovereignty. Regarding the trains, he roared that he would do what he considered most convenient. The consul's secretary repeated his orders mechanically, and Maass, after reiterating his decision not to allow the landing, hung up the phone. When he ended the call, his men warned him that the American troops were already at the docks and carrying out the landing in front of the train station. Only ten minutes had passed between the call and the landing.

According to his own report, Maass prepared to receive the invaders with heavy fire. The Americans, who possibly did not expect resistance, returned to their ships under a rain of shrapnel only to return a few moments later with all their force. Maass called Mexico City for instructions. Huerta, who wanted to avoid an open confrontation with the United States, ordered him to retreat ten miles inland. Before withdrawing, the 64-year-old general opened the jails. The army moved inland, but the students of the naval school organized the defense: they improvised barricades, and each cadet received 250 cartridges. Together with the prisoners and inhabitants of Veracruz, who went up to the rooftops with pistols, they prepared to defend the city. The fighting began at one o'clock in the afternoon.

Fletcher was a humanitarian who did not want to destroy the beautiful town of Veracruz, the oldest city in continental America, with its colonial churches, porticoes, cobbled streets, and houses full of flowers. On the third day, the far superior US forces captured the city and stationed there. Their intention was not to invade Mexico but to weaken the Huerta regime by cutting off its main source of income (the Veracruz customs) and, more importantly, impede its trade with Germany.

Despite the fact that many Mexicans viewed Huerta as "the jackal," throughout the country, the people rallied against the invasion. When President Wilson learned that Mexican civilians had resisted the occupation, which had resulted in the death of nineteen Americans and several hundred Mexicans, he was dismayed. In several parts of Mexico, many volunteers showed up to resist what they thought was a new war of conquest. Huerta tried to take advantage of that momentum, but it was not enough. He was fenced on all sides. The blockade of Veracruz benefited a new revolutionary chief and a friend of Madero's, Venustiano Carranza, the governor of Coahuila. After the assassination of the previous president, Carranza had issued his own Plan of Guadalupe to continue the Mexican Revolution. His proclamation was direct and brief. He declared that Huerta's government was illegitimate, as well as the legislative and judicial powers and the state governments. Carranza also expressed his intention to take command of an army, capture Mexico City, assume the presidency provisionally, and call for new elections.

Like the late Francisco Madero, Carranza was a northerner, a landowner, and a member of the upper class. He was 55 years old when he started his uprising. He was spirited and vigorous, but he wore a huge fluffy white beard and small round spectacles that made him look like an old Mexican Santa Claus. Pancho Villa called him goat-bearded. However, Carranza had such determination and energy that, in a short time, he gathered a big army and formed a true opposition against Huerta. Furthermore, Carranza attracted the interest of the United States. With more and more killings, repression, arrests, and forced conscription, even the skeptics were convinced that Victoriano Huerta had to go. "I will not recognize a government of butchers," President Wilson confided privately to a friend in May 1913.

Chapter 7 – Two Hurricanes

—When the Revolution is won, will you be the army?

—When the Revolution is won, there will be no more army. The men are sick of armies.

Journalist John Reed, interviewing revolutionary guerrillas

One of the most compelling metaphors to describe what happened next in the Mexican Revolution is that of a great wind that swept Mexico. With the exception of the two peninsulas in the east and west of the territory—Baja California and Yucatan, where the war barely touched people's lives—there was no place in the country to hide from the dust clouds raised by the warhorses, the gunshots of massive executions on both sides, the laments of a mother who had just seen her daughter abducted by the troops, or the wild screams of the soldiers plundering yet another town. President Huerta tried to negotiate with each revolutionary independently and sent envoys to ask them to lay down their arms. No one accepted. Thus began the most destructive stage of the Mexican Revolution. All of Mexico felt the birth pangs of a new nation that was still far from being born.

Thirsty for revenge after learning of Madero's death, and encouraged by his ideal of justice, Pancho Villa crossed the border back into Mexico on a rainy night in March of 1913. "That night," he later recorded, "I had eight men with me, we had no definite plan, but had decided to make for my old haunts in the Sierra Madre mountains, where I knew that I could find men to follow me. We had one sack of flour, two small packages of coffee and some salt." Villa and his men started ambushing Huerta's army, trying to get ammo and guns. "I told my men that the enemy had those things, and we must take them from him." Villa heard of Carranza's Plan of Guadalupe and joined the cause...for the moment.

By the following week, a hundred men were with him. A few months later, his popular army amounted to more than 18,000 troops, 30 cannons, and several machine guns. First, Villa conquered the state of Chihuahua, which was connected to the United States by train. Battle after battle, Villa took control of all of northern Mexico. He was ruthless with his prisoners of war, whose lives he only spared occasionally when his lieutenant, Felipe Ángeles, intervened, but he also showed a social consciousness. In 1913, he was the governor of Chihuahua for two months. In those eight weeks, he expropriated the property of the rich, confiscated gold from the banks, and established heavy taxes on the upper class; in return, he opened several schools, issued laws to protect widows and orphans, ordered the price of meat, milk, and bread to be lowered, and promised his soldiers and families that he would distribute the lands after their triumph of the Mexican Revolution. Villa set the price of meat at seven cents a pound, milk at five cents a liter, and a large piece of bread at four cents. On Christmas Day, he brought together all the poor of Chihuahua and gave fifteen pesos to each one. He sent his soldiers to patrol the streets, warning them that he would shoot anyone who got drunk or burglarized. There was no hunger in Chihuahua, and Villa became known as the "Friend of the Poor."

Contrary to the popular image of an uncontrolled man, Villa abhorred alcohol and vice. One of the first things he did after taking a city was to pour hundreds of liters of alcohol through the streets to keep his soldiers from falling into temptation. Governor Villa wasn't interested in exercising power behind a desk. In January 1914, he left the governorship, and two months later, he began his march south to

Mexico City, where Huerta was still sitting on the presidential chair. Meanwhile, his army, the famous Division of the North, attracted more volunteers. His conquests were unstoppable, and other generals of the Mexican Revolution began to see him with distrust and uneasiness. The men that followed Villa felt a mixture of admiration and fear, but they were encouraged by his willingness to reward those who were loyal. Legends were woven around the "Centaur of the North," as he was now called, and fantastic tales were told about his exploits.

John Reed, an American journalist who became a friend of Villa's, is one of our best sources for those days when the Centaur was the most popular man of Mexico and his Division of the North the most formidable army. On the field, Villa had to invent an entirely original method of warfare, which involved secrecy, quickness of movement, and the adaptation of his plans to the character of the country and of his soldiers. He established intimate relations with the rank and file, and he built up a superstitious belief among the enemy that his army was invincible and that Villa himself possessed a kind of talisman that made him immortal. He shot enemy officers immediately but spared the common soldiers and invited them to join the Division of the North.

John Reed was intimate with Villa. The Centaur of the North called him "Juanito," or Johnny. Reed observed how, when Villa's army went into battle, it was not hampered by salutes, trigonometrical calculations of the trajectories of projectiles, theories of the percentage of hits in a thousand rounds of rifle fire, or the function of cavalry, infantry, and artillery in any particular position. Villa did not know about those things, but he knew that his men could not be driven blindly in platoons around the field in perfect step because they were fighting individually and of their own free will. Reed thought they were braver than the old-fashioned federal army, whose men had been press-ganged. The journalist, surprised, saw how, when the revolutionaries rushed the streets of an ambushed town, Villa was among them like any common soldier.

Like the Northern Division, other armies during the Mexican Revolution brought hundreds of women soldiers and children with them. There are numerous historic photographs of women, some of them almost teenagers, shooting rifles. "Villa," wrote Reed, who witnessed the Division of the North in action, was "the first man to think of swift forced marches of bodies of cavalry, leaving their women behind. Up to his time no Mexican army had ever abandoned its base; it had always stuck closely to the railroad and the supply trains. But Villa struck terror into the enemy by abandoning his trains and throwing his entire effective army upon the field, as he did at Gómez Palacio [Durango, northern Mexico]. He invented in Mexico that most demoralizing form of battle—the night attack."

In the United States, his exploits were legendary. The Centaur of the North, whose main bases were close to the US border, was a practical man. He affirmed that he was a friend of the Americans. For a time, he was a kind of Mexican Robin Hood, whose adventures Hollywood wanted to glamorize. One of the strangest moments of the Mexican Revolution was when, in 1914, Villa reached an agreement with a film company, Mutual, to film his battles in order to make a movie so the American public would know the deeds of the famous general. Mutual Film Company made him wear a special uniform to make him look more lovable for the camera. "Is Villa a bandit or soldier, a Jesse James or a George Washington, a Robin Hood or a Napoleon, a robber, or a patriot and a hero?" asked *Reel Life* magazine in 1914, and then gave the answer: "Mutual cameramen, who have spent weeks in the field and who have come to know him well, declare that he is a misunderstood and much maligned man."

Mutual Film Company was granted exclusive rights to film Villa's troops in battle, and Villa would receive 20 percent of all revenues that the films produced. However, the footage was not good enough for the director, so Mutual decided to produce a new film from scratch. *The Life of General Villa*, duly sweetened for North

American audiences, was released in May 1914 without much fanfare.

Zapata

If there was a Centaur in the north, then there was an Attila in the south. That's the moniker that the virulent press of Mexico City gave to Emiliano Zapata, the peasant leader who fought for "Land and Freedom" for the rural workers.

His agenda was limited but clear. With the stubbornness of a rock, he defended it, unimpressed by promises of economic reforms or political freedom. The land came first, and there was no need to wait. Everything else would come in time. Zapata's peasants in arms were especially hated and feared in the capital. The press called them barbarians, savages from the mountain, and even polygamists. Ordinary people, based on what the newspapers fed them, believed that when Zapata's hordes reached the city, they would kill all the inhabitants and destroy civilization, especially when Zapata, the general with the huge sombrero and mustache, sent a war communique to Mexico City that read as the following:

At a council of war, it has been resolved to take Mexico City by fire and sword. Drastic justice will be done to all enemies, those responsible for criminal offenses will be executed by the military authorities. The property of the sentenced will be confiscated and sent for the support of the army. All the officers and commanders of the so-called federal army will be executed without a trial, since they are the only ones sustaining the usurper. Should they surrender before they are captured, and are not guilty of other crimes, they will be pardoned. The traitors Huerta and Blanquet will be degraded after a short trial and hanged from the balconies of the National Palace as a general warning. The remaining members of the cabinet will be shot following a summary trial. The lives and interests of foreigners will be respected if they are neutral. Five days will be given to the inhabitants of Mexico City who wish to avoid the horrors of war and [wish to] leave the city.

Signed — EMILIANO ZAPATA.

Every president, from Madero to de la Barra to Huerta, had placed great emphasis on destroying the most radical wing of the Mexican Revolution represented by Zapata. Huerta was particularly brutal, punishing the civilian population of the towns that supported or hid Zapatistas. Entire villages were burned. A witness of the time left a vivid description of Zapata's men and women:

They were a revolving peasant army, based on their own homes. The soldiers went back from time to time to look after their corn and chili patches. A detachment could, if in an inconvenient military spot, simply evaporate, each man becoming again a soft-eyed, vague-talking peasant by just slipping off his cartridge belt and putting it with his gun in a cache. It was impossible to defeat them, difficult even to find them, as they materialized only when they were ready to attack; and knew, besides, all the shortcuts in their mountain country. They wore ordinary peasant white, except the chiefs who dressed in ranchero clothes; in Zapata's case, symbolic, theatrical, dead-black, skintight and set off with startling silver. The first act on raiding a hacienda or municipal center was sharp and symbolic: they got to the safe and destroyed all papers dealing with land titles, and then invited the neighborhood peasants to homestead on the hacienda lands.

In any case, the loyalty that Zapata aroused among his men was as intense or perhaps more than that of Villa. Both generals were advancing toward the center of Mexico, to the country's capital, where the two titans would meet.

The Battle of Zacatecas: The Deadly Blow to Huerta

The fall of Victoriano Huerta was a direct consequence of Pancho Villa's victories and his Division of the North. The articles by John Reed, who later went on to write a famous book on the Russian Revolution, are invaluable firsthand materials to help one appreciate the drawing power and near-mythical status of Villa during his moments of glory in 1914. It was "the most satisfying moment of my life," Reed wrote as he advanced with the largest army in Mexico toward the capital. He was not a reporter in the traditional sense. He became part of the lives of the revolutionary men and women in order to see the conflict from their point of view. Reed took sides with them to experience the promise of a free nation where there would be no underclass, oppressive army, or dictators.

Reed witnessed how people worshiped Villa even when he was not around. The soldiers composed *corridos* to the Centaur of the North—a musical genre, or war songs of the Mexican Revolution. Next to a fire, the reporter was delighted as a man began to sing a verse from "Francisco Villa's morning song," and then the man next to him composed the following on the spot. Each one contributed to a dramatic tale of the general's exploits for more than three hours.

Your tamer has arrived, Pancho Villa the fighter, to kick you out of Torreón and to remove even your skin!

The rich with their money, they got a good blow from the soldiers of Urbina and those of Maclovio Herrera too.

Fly, fly, little dove, fly over the meadows, tell everybody that Villa has come to make them run.

Ambition will be ruined, and justice will win, as Villa came to Torreón to punish the greedy.

Fly, fly, golden eagle, take these laurels to Villa, for he has come to conquer Bravo and his colonels.

Now beware, sons of the mosquito, Villa has arrived in Torreón, to deal with the evil deeds of all those damned baldies [the federal soldiers].

Long live Villa and his soldiers! Long live Herrera and his people! Now you know, wicked people, what a brave man can do.

Other famous *corridos* among the Division of the North, such as "La Adelita" and "La Valentina," both tales about women, were preserved and recorded multiple times.

If Adelita left with another man
I would follow her by land and by sea.
If by sea, on a warship
If by land, on a military train.

"La Valentina" is a love song for a young woman showing the fatalistic attitude of the Villistas:

If they're going to kill me tomorrow,

let them kill me at once.

When Villa left Chihuahua, he cut the telegraph wires communicating to the north and forbade, on pain of death, that anyone should carry or send news of his departure. He wanted to take the federal army by surprise. The first serious blow to Huerta was the capture of the city of Torreón. Torreón was an essential railway hub where Villa could control important resources. From that point onward, he let the soldiers' wives accompany them on the trains to cook and sometimes to join the fight, which further increased his army. When Villa boarded his trains with his Northern Division, the scene seemed like an exodus. The next target was Zacatecas, the geographic center of Mexico.

Venustiano Carranza, the chief with the white beard and round spectacles, began feeling jealous of Villa's power and popularity. Carranza ordered the Centaur to put himself under the orders of General Álvaro Obregón. Because Carranza knew that Zacatecas was the strategic point of entry to the south, he ordered Villa to withdraw and desist, but the Centaur ignored the orders. On June 23rd, 1914, in what had been one of the richest cities in colonial Mexico, thanks to its gold and silver mines, the decisive battle of the Mexican Revolution began. Rebel troops attacked from all sides with cavalry charges and cannon fire from the hills. Federal soldiers panicked, got rid of their uniforms, and hid in houses, while a few fled south, where fresh revolutionary troops were waiting for them and took them down from both sides of the road. In one of the bloodiest actions, one of the city's defenders blew up an ammunition depot rather than let it fall into Villa's hands. The explosion destroyed an entire block and left hundreds of dead civilians. Altogether, more than 7,000 military and civilian lives were lost in a single day.

In one year, the Mexican Revolution had left Huerta with only a fraction of the country. However, the opposition to Huerta was far from being a unified movement fighting for a common cause. The only thing that united the armies of the south, north, and northwest was their desire to overthrow the dictator. Although the north of Mexico initially presented a united front, disagreements soon separated the leaders, and none of them recognized the other as the leader of the revolution. Each major general had his own political and, in some cases, economic and foreign agendas, which did not necessarily coincide. There only seemed to be a current of sympathy with Pancho Villa and Emiliano Zapata, since both were peasants and represented the radical, popular wing of the revolution. Although Carranza, a high-class landowner, also wanted to overthrow Huerta, he had more conservative plans.

Good-bye to Huerta

The country no longer belonged to Huerta or to the old Porfiristas. For a critical moment, it belonged to no one; it was a house divided and destroyed by forces financed by different interests. In 1914, during the negotiations in Niagara Falls, which took place there in order to avoid war between the United States and Mexico and which involved the intercession of the ABC countries (Argentina, Brazil, and Chile), the representatives agreed to the end of the US occupation of Veracruz with the condition that Huerta give up. The old general could have stayed and allied himself with other powers, but the country was no longer his; it now belonged to a new generation of revolutionary leaders. On July 15th, the president finally resigned before Mexico's Congress and headed to Veracruz to board the German steamer SS *Dresden* that would take him to Europe. Three years earlier, he had escorted Porfirio Díaz to the same place to board another German steamer that disappeared into the Atlantic. Now, he was following the same destiny. But unlike Don Porfirio, Huerta would not go as a tourist to see the pyramids of Egypt and the Champs-Élysées. On the outside, he looked as decrepit as Díaz, but Huerta was not an old man: he was only 64.

When he submitted his resignation to Congress, the dictator delivered an enigmatic message. With his eagle gaze, he reminded the audience that his solemn promise had been to make peace in Mexico, and for this, he had formed an army. He reminded them about the scarcity of resources he had faced and how "a great power on this continent" had supported the rebels. He mentioned the occupation in Veracruz and the agreements they had reached in the Niagara Peace Conference, and he said that his government had dealt a deathblow to an unjust power. "Robust workers will come later with more perfect tools that will annihilate, without a doubt, that power that has caused so much damage and [is responsible for] so many attacks on this continent." The newspapers reproduced Huerta's speech but were puzzled, not knowing what to do with the message. The old president had not even scratched the United States. Possibly, beneath his prophetic tone, there were other plans that were just materializing in his mind. Huerta, whom everyone considered at the time to be no more than a living corpse, still had a plan. He still wanted to save his country.

Chapter 8 – The Convention of Aguascalientes

Besides Villa, Zapata, and Carranza, there were other leaders in the corners of the country. There was Álvaro Obregón, a former chickpea farmer who had assembled his own army made up of the fierce Yaqui of Sonora. Álvaro Obregón, the rising star in 1914, had a peculiar history. He had lost his father as a child, and his family had moved to a swampy coastal area populated mainly by the Mayo people, where the young Álvaro (whose name means "always prudent") grew up in poverty. There, he learned the language of the Mayo and became a staunch defender of Native American rights. As he was growing up, he worked as a mechanic, barber, painter, teacher, door-to-door shoe salesman, and even as a musician. At the age of 26, he finally tried to grow chickpeas and started exporting crops to the US, and he became a prosperous farmer. When he joined the Mexican Revolution in 1912, his most loyal followers were the Mayo and Yaqui of Sonora, whom he had defended so much throughout his life and whose language he spoke. Obregón was athletic and good-looking, with thick eyebrows and a soft gaze. He considered himself a socialist and led the Constitutional Army of the

Northwest, in the same region as Pancho Villa, in support of Carranza. But loyalties could, and often did, shift.

Other chiefs moved separately without responding to anyone. With no president of the republic, no elections on the horizon, and an entire country up in arms, the only thing left was anarchy and chaos. There were so many leaders, each with a different idea of what Mexico should be, and some of them simply abandoned their beliefs to the game of looting, destruction, and endless fighting. The movement started by Francisco Madero in 1910 threatened to disintegrate the country.

Venustiano Carranza, the self-appointed "first chief of the Revolution," considered that it was time to make a truce and sit everyone down to talk. It was for that reason that he called a meeting in the city of Aguascalientes, a neutral territory 100 kilometers (about 62 miles) south of Zacatecas. Aguascalientes was then a quiet city, famous for its hot springs and its exotic public garden dedicated to Saint Mark. Its orchards of figs, pears, peaches, and grapes girded the city like a belt, despite the fact that the town was located on arid land. It was time, said Carranza, to pass from arms to proposals, to define the country they wanted. The Convention of Aguascalientes was a moment of good judgment and hope in the midst of a country that was heading to chaos.

As the troops approached the shining city, which had remained free from the turmoil of the Mexican Revolution, an air of apprehension ran through the streets. The owners of the inns and taverns worked overtime. The only two hotels in the city were sold out even before the trains began to arrive with the delegates. The hostels were converted into barracks, and many wealthy families had to offer accommodation, not without some apprehension, to military personnel, expecting some protection in return. In the homes where there were unmarried girls, their parents hastily sent them out of town. As for the other family treasures—gold, jewelry, silver coins— the inhabitants of Aguascalientes hid them under their ovens or buried them next to a tree in the backyard.

On October 10th, 1914, the city became the nation's military, political, and nervous center when delegates from Villa, Carranza, and other chiefs began arriving at the Morelos Theater, the headquarters of the Convention. In its inaugural session, 115 soldiers were registered for the debate. The entire republic was attentive to what would be said there. But the Zapatistas were missing, and therefore, the assembly was incomplete, like a car without one of its wheels. General Felipe Ángeles, Villa's most trusted military man, asked that the corps extend an invitation to the men from the south, adding that the Division of the North was in a position to make a complete peace in the country because Villa was in agreement with Zapata.

In an unexpected move, when the Convention began its sessions, it declared itself sovereign and was, therefore, the highest authority in the country. This meant that it was self-vested with absolute power and that it would only respond to itself. One of the generals spoke up and set the tone: "We did not come to discuss whether Carranza or Villa should be president. We came to do a government program and we want peace. We want justice! And know it well: we are not afraid of any of the armies." One by one, the representatives of the armed factions walked on stage to sign the flag that Álvaro Obregón, the former chickpea planter, had brought from Mexico City. When they stamped their signature on the cloth, each general, military man, and chief said these words: "Before this flag, for my honor as an armed citizen, I protest to carry out the decisions of this assembly."

General Felipe Ángeles insisted that the Convention was not complete without Zapata's envoys, and he offered to go on an expedition to the south to bring them. "Gentlemen, let's say to Zapata: Redeemer of the peasants, come here, brother, that there are many arms that want to embrace yours." His proposal was echoed with thunderous applause, and the sober general went south in search of the elusive Zapata. None of the three great men of the Mexican Revolution at that time—Villa, Zapata, or Carranza— were present in the audience. Carranza, not quite humbly, had said that his presence could influence the deliberations and therefore would not attend the meeting. Villa was nearby with his army, a few miles away, in the town of Guadalupe. Zapata had said that he would not go unless they accepted his Plan of Ayala without changing an iota of it.

Actually, the chiefs were being too cautious. They knew that treason was lurking around the corner. However, on October 17th, a distinguished guest appeared in the city: Pancho Villa. He was going to sign the Convention's flag. There is only one photograph of the moment. General Villa, well-groomed and spotless in a new suit, is signing with his right hand. Behind him, four other delegates witness the scene. None of them looks at the camera or at Villa. Since the Division of the North was on the outskirts of Aguascalientes, many delegates feared that there would be a violent takeover, but the Centaur signed and departed, respecting the city.

Illustration 3. Villa signing the flag during the Convention of Aguascalientes. Unknown photographer, 1914. Fondo Casasola, INAH, Mexico.

The Zapatistas Make Their Entrance

On October 27th, the most expected guests arrived at the assembly. The Zapatistas went down to Aguascalientes from the southern mountains. Amidst applause, the commission walked in the theater, and thus, the most mature ideological movement joined the discussions. The spirit of national unity excited everyone. The Convention was, from that moment on, the most authoritative institution of the Mexican Revolution. The Zapatista delegation was made up of seasoned intellectuals with a defined ideological stance. "We regret this division existing among those of us who rose together in 1910 to overthrow a dictatorship that we believed to be invincible," began Paulino Martínez, the leader of the Zapatista delegation, a small man with a formidable mustache who had been an opposition journalist from the Porfirio Díaz era. "We sincerely deplore that our comrades today are perhaps going to be the enemies that we'll fight tomorrow. We do not want this fratricidal struggle." And then, he presented the content of the Plan of Ayala.

Tierra y Libertad, land and freedom is what synthesizes our plan for the economic freedom of the Mexican people...not privileges for a certain social group, but political equality and collective well-being for all the inhabitants of the republic; [we want] a home for each family, a piece of bread for each destitute person, a light for each brain in the school-farms that the Revolution will establish after the victory, and land for all, because the extension of the Mexican territory can comfortably house ninety to one hundred million inhabitants.

The crowd erupted in applause.

The next Zapatista speaker, Antonio Díaz Soto y Gama, an incendiary orator, walked to the podium and, in mid-speech, grabbed the Mexican flag that everyone had signed with one quick movement. To everyone's surprise, he squeezed it contemptuously and said he would never sign that flag that had waved in the sumptuous buildings of the tyrants. "The word of honor is worth more than a signature," he snapped. More than 200 pistols came out of their holsters, and for a moment, the tension reached unfathomable levels. Soto y Gama stood there without flinching, unmoved. A few women in the upper floor passed out. Desperate, the president of the Convention urged everyone to calm down, reminding them that one shot would be enough to ruin what was being accomplished there. An eyewitness later recalled how people from the upper floors (civilians) rushed to the exit, screaming, pushing each other, and rolling down the stairs, but they were stopped at the entrance by the guards.

A few days after the flag incident, a movie about the Mexican Revolution was shown at the theater. Many Conventionists were amazed because it was the first time in their lives that they had seen a movie. The columns of Yaqui soldiers appeared, then a sequence of General Álvaro Obregón (who was present in the audience), and trains, while the public gaped at the human figures made of shadow and light. The movie seemed so real that when Venustiano Carranza on horseback appeared on the screen for the hundredth time, solemn and expressionless as he entered Mexico City, some shouted, "Death to Carranza!" took out their pistols, and shot the screen. The anecdote was narrated by the Mexican novelist Martín Luis Guzmán, who was also present. Being a civilian, he had slipped through the back door with a friend and sat behind the screen, so they were watching the movie from the other side of the cloth. The bullets landed directly on Carranza's chest and passed just above their heads. "If Carranza had entered Mexico City on foot," Guzmán wrote, "the bullets would have been for us."

The next resolution of the Convention caught the three great leaders by surprise: the delegates asked Carranza, Villa, and Zapata to relinquish command of their respective armies, which were holding the country captive. From Mexico City, Carranza telegraphed that he would resign as the First Chief only if Pancho Villa renounced his Northern Division first and retired into private life. Carranza could not tolerate Villa's independence and autonomy, the strength of his army, the radical social reforms that he had launched in Chihuahua, and the fact that Villa publicly opposed his foreign policy. When he heard that Carranza would resign if he did so as well, the Centaur sent a remarkable counterproposal: "I propose that both of us, the goat-bearded and I, be shot!"

Chapter 9 – The Presidential Chair

The Aguascalientes Convention was, for a few weeks, pregnant with hope, a first parliamentary school in the new Mexico. Since the times of the Congress that had drafted the Constitution of 1857, there had not been an unrestricted and open debate because Porfirio Díaz had had a Congress filled with puppets. But the assembly was not yet over when the armies had moved on to their business again. They had guns at their disposal, and the temptation to use them was great. In the north, General Maclovio Herrera rebelled against Pancho Villa. "That big-eared scoundrel!" Villa thundered. "How could he? I made him! He is my son in arms! How dare that deaf and ungrateful traitor abandon me?" At the Aguascalientes Convention, attempts were made to reconcile interests, but the real politics were something else. The assembly had been divided into two irreconcilable camps, those with Pancho Villa and those with Carranza.

Looking for an intermediate point, the Aguascalientes Convention named a virtual unknown as the president of the republic, General Eulalio Gutiérrez, who, in turn, appointed Villa as the supreme military chief of the new government. It was obvious then who was controlling the deliberations. Cautious, the young ex-farmer Obregón avoided identifying with Carranza. He was sailing where the wind blew. In Mexico City, the chief with the long white beard packed his bags and left for the city of Puebla, having learned of the imminent arrival of the Division of the North. In the south, Zapata's men also began their march toward the capital. They were like two hurricanes that were going to meet in the center. In Mexico City, panic spread because the press depicted the Zapatistas as savages and Zapata as a barbaric and bloodthirsty Attila. Hotels, restaurants, cafés, and drugstores closed their doors, and people locked themselves in their homes. Some students took up arms to defend the city from "the barbarians."

But when the so-called barbarians arrived on November 24th, 1914, the people were stunned. It was a crowd of peasants, most of them indigenous, in white cotton pants, some of them riding starving horses. Some carried machetes, others had rifles, and very few had Remingtons. They covered their heads with large palm hats, wore huaraches, and marched with large numbers of women, some of them very young, almost girls dressed as men, and carrying rifles. Many spoke indigenous languages, not Spanish, and brought banners of the Virgin of Guadalupe. Spontaneously, people started clapping and throwing flowers at them. Contrary to expectations, the Zapatista leaders reestablished order in Mexico City after Carranza's departure, and instead of looting the stores, the men and women went from house to house, knocking on doors and asking for food. A few days later, the Northern Division arrived. General Felipe Ángeles established his headquarters in the Chapultepec Castle, awaiting the advent of General Villa, who arrived by train in early December.

The two great popular leaders, Pancho Villa and Emiliano Zapata, met for the first time in Xochimilco, on the outskirts of Mexico City. They gave each other a warm hug, and the people who witnessed the scene burst into applause, as the north and south were finally meeting. They had both heard of each other. Zapata, who was not much given to express his feelings, understood that Villa, the expropriator of the large estates in Chihuahua, was the only chief who would support his agrarian program. They sat at a table to enjoy a meal consisting of turkey, tamales, and beans with epazote. A secretary who was present at the meal recorded the dialogue between the two leaders for posterity.

Villa: I do not want government positions because I do not know how to "deal" [with bureaucratic matters]. Let's see how we can find these [the right] people. We're just going to warn them not to give us headaches.

Zapata: That's why I warn all these folks to be very careful, otherwise the machete will go down on their heads. (Laughter.) Well, I know that we won't be deceived. We have been limiting ourselves to herd them, to watch them very very closely, to take care of them, and to keep them quiet as well.

Villa: I very well understand that we the ignorant men make the war, and the cabinets take advantage of us; [it's ok] as long as they don't cause us any more trouble.

Zapata: The men who work harder are the least who should enjoy the sidewalks [the luxuries of the city]. I see no more than sidewalks [here]. And I say to myself: when I walk on a sidewalk, I get dizzy and I want to fall.

Villa: This little ranch [Mexico City] is very big for us; it's much better out there [in the fields]. As soon as this is arranged, I'll leave for the Northern campaign. I have a lot to do there. The fight is going to be very hard over there. I'm a man who doesn't like to flatter; but you know, I've been thinking about you for a long time.

Zapata: Likewise. Those who have traveled to the North, the many people who have gone over there, those who have approached you, they must have informed you that I had big hopes on you. Villa is, I said, the only true person, and the war will continue, because as far as I'm concerned, they [the men in power] don't want to make anything right, and I will continue until the day I die.

At the Presidential Chair
Both chiefs agreed that they would enter Mexico City at the same hour and meet at the National Palace on December 6th, 1914. Villa

wore a new high-rank uniform, Zapata, a charro suit. There is a film of Villa and Zapata at a banquet that took place at the Palace, but the film lasts for only a few seconds. In the film, one can see, sitting in the middle of them with a suit, tie, and spectacles, the Convention's president, Eulalio Gutiérrez. To his right is Villa, and Zapata is on his left. Zapata, who is visibly the tallest of the three, looks down and eats, leans toward his plate, and touches his face when the camera passes in front of him. Eulalio Gutiérrez moves nervously and gives orders to his assistants; to his right, Villa chews enthusiastically without paying attention to the cameraman, chatting and laughing. The truly iconic moment came later that day when they assembled at the president's office to see the presidential chair. "Is that the chair they fight so much about?" Villa asked mockingly.

A historic photograph of both men at the chair was captured by Agustín Casasola. In it, Villa and Zapata are surrounded by a motley crowd, including some children and a man with a bandaged head. By this point, they were two living legends. The photo is anti-solemn. Villa's laughter, frozen in time, shows that he is delighted. Zapata, who rarely left his southern domains, isn't smiling. "Sit down, my general, please," said Villa, taking off his cap and stretching his arm. "No, you first," said Zapata. "But please, the honor belongs to you," Villa insisted, amused. "No, I'd rather not sit," said Zapata, "because when someone is good and sits on that chair, when he gets up, he is bad."

Illustration 4. Villa and Zapata share the presidential chair.
Photograph by Agustín Casasola, 1914.
Fototeca INAH, Mexico.

Although Villa and Zapata might have seen the occasion and the ensuing photograph as a souvenir or something to boast about back home, like a hunter with his foot on a dead lion's head, what was happening there was actually unprecedented: for the first time in Mexico's history, the people were in power. The leaders of the revolution had reached their highest point, and they could have ordered whatever they wanted at the moment—the immediate return of the land to the peasants, to improve the workers' conditions, the betterment of the urban classes. But this idea of becoming the person with all the control clashed with the apathy and unwillingness of both leaders, who were more interested in their limited worlds than being presidents of Mexico. Other historians believe that Villa, considering himself an ignorant and unprepared man, was psychologically defeated. Casasola's photo marked the apex of Villa's career and, for that very same reason, the beginning of his decline.

Zapata had never considered living in the city and becoming a bureaucrat, let alone the nation's president. "General Zapata, stretching his face with a kind smile, showed appreciation to the acclamations with slight bows of his head," wrote Francisco Ramírez Plancarte 25 years later in his memoirs, a man who witnessed the historic moment. As Villa and Zapata reviewed the troops from the balcony of the National Palace on the only occasion they met, Zapata's "gaze was peaceful, laying his sweet and vague eyes on the agitated sea of faces." Zapata and Villa would never meet again.

Chapter 10 – Huerta Strikes Back

"Whenever war occurs in any part of the world,
   we in Germany sit down and make a plan."
—Kaiser Wilhelm II

"There is vestige of hope in the report that Huerta left his exile in Spain and has gone to America. This strong man could save the country if anybody could."
—*Frankfurten Zeitung,* April 15, 1915

The exiled and overthrown president, Victoriano Huerta, boarded a German steamer to England. From there, he went to Spain. The man with the perpetual scowl arrived in Barcelona in August 1914, three days before the start of the First World War. During the first days of his arrival, tired and in poor health, he dedicated himself to recovering, but he was following the development of the Mexican Revolution with great interest.

In Spain, he came across an elusive German spy and conspirator called Franz von Rintelen, a 38-year-old naval officer whose mission was to open a secret front in Mexico against the United States. "I had studied the foreign political situation in the United States and realized that the only country it should fear was Mexico," Rintelen wrote in his memoirs. "If Mexico attacked, the US would need to use all the ammunition it could make, and it could not export arms to Europe." Rintelen found Huerta and offered the help of Kaiser Wilhelm II to lead a revolution in Mexico and regain his presidency. Huerta must have smirked and put aside his eternal scowl for a few seconds because he had never once abandoned the idea of returning to Mexico. The fractures among the revolutionaries must have appeared to him as the perfect opportunity to reestablish a strong regime that would have the support of the army and the weary upper and middle classes who were tired of war.

Von Rintelen was serving as the head of the German Secret Service in the US, and he was possibly the most important German spy of the time. In just a few months of his arrival in America, he had successfully exploded fifty Allied ships at sea, staged strikes at American ports, destroyed a New York dock full of weapons bound for Russia, and blown up the Canadian Automobile and Foundry Company. With almost unlimited resources and ample decision-making ability, Rintelen was doing in America what other Germans were doing in the Middle East: fomenting local wars that would distract the resources of the enemy powers. If Mexico were to become a threat to the United States, the US would have to deploy its resources on its own continent and leave Germany alone in Europe. On the other hand, if Germany had an ally in the Americas, it could use Mexico's territory to launch more effective aggression. Ultimately, the Kaiser hoped to convince Mexico to declare war on the United States.

In America, the city of El Paso had become a hotbed of Mexican exiles who, concerned about anarchy in their country and the seemingly endless bloodbath, were conspiring to intervene, take over, and reestablish order. Through an organization called the "Mexican Peace Assembly," they pointed out the excesses of the revolution and compared them to those committed during France's Reign of Terror. At the head of the conspiracy was General Pascual Orozco, who had been one of the first to respond to Francisco Madero's call and was later exiled to the United States. Their dilemma was not only the lack of resources but the lack of a strong figure capable of uniting broad sectors of Mexican society. General Orozco sent Enrique Creel, a member of one of the most powerful families in Mexico during the Porfiriato, to talk with Huerta in Spain.

Creel arrived at the right time, which was one month after the Huerta-Von Rintelen interview. The stars were aligned for Victoriano. The former dictator had accepted German aid, and that same month, he returned to America with Creel in the steamer *López*. In April 1915, when the Mexican Revolution had hit rock-bottom, with the Aguascalientes Convention having failed and the all-out war between Villa and Carranza, Huerta landed in New York, where the press and a handful of enthusiastic admirers rushed to greet him. The man stated that he was on a leisure trip to the United States. Both the representatives of Villa and Carranza in the US protested to the Wilson government for allowing Huerta to disembark in New York, but the old general had his papers in order. In a Manhattan café, the Mexican national anthem was played when they saw that Huerta was there. In the following days, he told the press that a strong man would soon appear to take the reins of destiny in his country, although he did not say who.

For a few weeks, New York became the center of the counter-revolution. Meetings with the German embassy staff were held secretly at the Manhattan Hotel in Broadway, where Huerta met with Rintelen, German Naval Attaché Karl Boy-Ed, and Franz von Papen, a general who had served in the Imperial German Army since he was eighteen and had been sent to organize acts of sabotage in the United States. American intelligence knew about these meetings. Huerta, informed of the Orozco conspiracy and the Peace Assembly, commented to Rintelen that the situation in Mexico was so serious that it defied description, and he requested financing of one million dollars. The agreement was finalized that same month. The Germans deposited almost the whole amount in two bank accounts in Mexico and Cuba, and they promised that German U-boats would deliver weapons to different points on the Mexican coast. It was also stipulated that when Huerta became president again, Germany would support him in both war and peace. On June 1ˢ, 1915, Huerta met with important Mexican exiles at the Holland House hotel. One of them was a spy for Carranza, who telegrammed Mexico that the former president had ten million dollars for his coup, plus the double of that amount in reserve. Finally, Pascual Orozco arrived in Manhattan, finalized details with Huerta, and set June 28ᵗʰ as the date for the invasion.

When the weapons for the conspiracy began to cross into Mexico, the American spies, cognizant of Huerta's footsteps, sent frantic reports to their own government. Two days before the appointed date, Huerta took a train to El Paso, where all the Mexican exiles began to arrive from different parts of the United States. Huerta and General Orozco set the small town of Newman, ten miles north of El Paso, as a meeting point, from where they would ride to Mexico. Everything was ready. At the last minute, Huerta and Orozco were arrested by agents of the US Department of Justice a few blocks away from the Mexican border. "I am now at your orders, gentlemen," said Huerta, without opposing resistance. As the news spread, a crowd gathered outside the El Paso prison, and fearing a diplomatic incident, Huerta was transferred to Fort Bliss. From his compartment in the fort, he sent for help from his alleged protectors. The telegram to Johann von Bernstorff, the German ambassador to the United States, said:

I am in Fort Bliss and my household consisting of thirty to thirty-five persons who are at the city of El Paso are not accorded guarantees of any kind. I wish to know whether the government of His Imperial Majesty, that you so worthily represent in Washington, can do me the favor of protecting my wife and children as the federal officers of the American Justice in this city do not let them sleep or eat and search my house at will. I respectfully beg your reply.

Victoriano Huerta

Germany ignored Huerta's call for help. In December, Franz von Papen and Karl Boy-Ed were expelled from the United States for conspiracy, and on January 13th, the old general died in his house after several operations without anesthesia at the Fort Bliss hospital. Huerta, who had appeared out of nowhere in the Tragic Ten Days, disappeared from history once again. Had he been successful—and there was a good possibility of this if he had crossed the border—he could have changed the history of the Western Hemisphere. For years, rumors circulated that he was poisoned or killed on the operating table. Victoriano Huerta now rests in a cemetery in El Paso in a humble grave.

Chapter 11 – The Horsemen of the Apocalypse

"I feel it to be my duty to tell them that, if they cannot accommodate their differences and unite for this great purpose within a very short time, this Government will be constrained to decide what means should be employed by the United States in order to help Mexico save herself and serve her people."

—US President Wilson to Villa and Carranza, May 1915

The Aguascalientes Convention came to nothing. The meetings of the assembly moved to Mexico City, but it was not even the shadow of the spirit of 1914. Virtually all of the delegates of Carranza and Villa had withdrawn and were again killing themselves in fields and ravines. In 1915, with an insurmountable wall between the two men, the war spread throughout the country, and the haciendas and cultivated fields were swept away again by the revolution. The country began to resent the effects of five years of war, and famine made itself present. As each faction began printing its own money to cover war expenses, prices went up exorbitantly. Carranza printed banknotes of his provisional government, Villa issued his own money, and Zapata minted coins. According to the region, or the fortune of each general, the bills were either accepted or rejected by the stores.

Given the abundance of worthless paper money, which the populace called "sheets" or "bilimbiques," people returned to bartering. In the days of the most acute inflation in 1915, a worker's day's wages could barely buy a kilo (2.2 pounds) of potatoes. Groups of desperate women stormed the meetings of the Convention with empty baskets. A delegate stood up and proposed to organize a collection to send them away with some money, but the protesters shouted that they wanted bread, not paper. Thinking about how to alleviate hunger, the Convention set up an aid station downtown to distribute corn to the population. When the news broke, thousands of people ran to the Palacio de Minería and flooded the courtyards. There was such chaos that people had to be dispersed with bullets. By mid-1915, groups of women walked the markets with empty baskets, only to find the stores were closed. Some people began tearing down the doors of the shops with axes and sticks, and the store owners defended their properties, shooting from the rooftops. Obregón even threatened to shoot the merchants who hid basic goods.

That same year, a typhoid epidemic struck the center of the country due to malnutrition, lack of personal and environmental hygiene, and poverty. Sometimes people would collapse in the middle of the street, their stomachs empty or their body ravaged by typhoid. The destruction and blockade of roads by the opposing armies, which interrupted the supply of goods to Mexico City, did not help. Every new army that occupied the capital— first Carranza, then Villa and Zapata, then Obregón, then Zapata again—depleted its meager reserves, aggravated the situation, and produced thousands of beggars and orphans in the streets.

The End of the Division of the North

To the relief of many, the most intense period of the civil war came to an end in the year 1915, the "year of hunger," with a massive bloodbath in central Mexico, where Pancho Villa suffered a series of defeats against the rising star, General Álvaro Obregón.

First, Obregón defeated the Zapatistas in Puebla and entered Mexico City. He let his beard grow and said he would not cut it until Villa was liquidated. Obregón took other cities in the center of the country, getting closer and closer to the Centaur, who also yearned for the final showdown so he could wipe out Obregón's army and then destroy the rest of Carranza's forces. Both titans met in the surroundings of the city of Celaya. The shooting started at four o'clock in the afternoon, and the fighting lasted for the rest of the day and all of the following night. Obregón telegraphed to the venerable-looking Carranza, "The assaults of the enemy are very crude. As long as a soldier and a bullet remain, I will know how to do my duty." At dawn, the Villistas tried again and again, without success, to storm the plaza until Obregón mobilized two powerful groups of cavalry to envelop the attackers from the south and the north. The Division of the North, which had no reserves, withdrew orderly at first and then in complete disarray. "The Villistas have left the field strewn with corpses," Obregón reported.

In the following days, Obregón got reinforcements, and his troops reached 15,000 soldiers. Villa's more experienced generals advised him to avoid the combat and retreat north, as the terrain was uneven and full of trench holes, but Villa still felt invincible. On April 13th, he attacked again, now with greater momentum, looking for a weak point in the defense. The Villistas depleted their force in fruitless assaults, and two days later, when the Centaur had already been fighting for 36 hours, Obregón ordered a counteroffensive. Mexican journalist Anita Brenner, who wrote one of the first histories of the Mexican Revolution in 1938, left a dramatic description of the final battle:

Against Villa's massive cavalry attacks, Obregon's strategy was to advance very fast, stop at some good fortifiable point, set up barbed wire entanglements and lay out trenches, in open loop shape, in which he put chiefly the Yaqui troops who were the core of his personal army. They had been fighting for generations, trained to win or commit suicide. When the fight began, the Yaquis lay each one in a trench-hole with his wife and children, who kept handing him a reloaded gun as fast as one was finished, and if he was wounded or killed, they continued firing. Cavalry issued to charge head-on into the Dorados [Villistas], and then to run apparently routed, into the open loop, where the Yaquis caught the pursuing Dorados in murderous crossfire. They massacred the first wave and the second and sometimes a third. The same sort of trap closed on them in battle after battle.

Before retreating like a wounded animal, Villa had one last gift for General Obregón. In the heat of battle, a grenade hit Obregón and blew off his right arm. Seeing himself mutilated like that, the handsome general pulled out his gun to commit suicide, but his weapon was unloaded, as his aide had forgotten to load it that day. Although he was out of combat for a few days, Obregón returned to finish off the invincible Northern Division, as he had promised, in the battles of León and Aguascalientes. There, he obliterated the bulk of Villa's forces and acquired a new nickname: El Manco de Celaya (the one-armed man of Celaya). His amputated hand, which the doctor kept in formalin inside a jar, would go on to have a bizarre adventure. Meanwhile, the former chickpea planter saw his star reach its zenith and finally shaved his beard, while Villa, with the remnants of his army, retreated north in a sad parade. He was not a threat to Carranza anymore.

After Celaya, as rumors grew that Villa had been defeated, that he had become more brutal, and that Germany had approached the Centaur with offers, the United States gave official recognition to Venustiano Carranza's "pre-constitutional government." With somewhat reluctant acceptance, US President Wilson hoped to stop the civil war to the south of the US border. In May 1917, without opposition, Carranza won the presidential election.

Villa was furious, but most of all, he was incredulous. He had always ordered to respect American property, had always had a favorable attitude toward the United States, had made friends with American reporters and filmmakers, and had even looked the other way during the occupation of the port of Veracruz in 1914. "I emphatically declare that I have much to thank Mr. Wilson for," Villa told a reporter, "because this now relieves me of the obligation to give guarantees to foreigners, and especially to those who once were free citizens and are now vassals of an evangelist Philosophy professor. Therefore, I decline all responsibility in the future." His words were a genuine and grim warning.

Chapter 12 – The Centaur and the General: Pershing's Punitive Expedition

Defeated by Obregón's forces, betrayed by the United States, and abandoned by his generals who were deserting him, including the prized general Felipe Ángeles, the architect of his triumphs and moderator of his tantrums, Villa's worst side took possession of him. The man, who has been described as both a compassionate angel and a butcher, had reason to feel like a cornered beast. In early 1916, with Venustiano Carranza in possession of Mexico, Villa was now reduced to a fugitive wandering through northern Mexico in search of provisions; he was no more than a bandit. The newspapers that previously praised him referred to him and his last faithful soldiers (the famous Dorados) as mere desperados.

On January 10th, the Villistas derailed a passenger train that was heading to a mining town called Cusihuiriachi (Cusi, for short). The train was transporting eighteen Americans who had been invited by the Mexican government to reopen some mines. The Villistas boarded the train, shot some of the Americans in cold blood while they were still in their seats, and stole their money. Others were taken off and shot on the spot. Only one American businessman, who played dead, survived and was able to reach Chihuahua to tell about the massacre. When the citizens of El Paso found out what had happened, they were so furious that the authorities had to declare martial law to prevent them from going to kill Mexicans across the river.

Two months later, on March 9th, 1916, at three o'clock in the morning, Villa crossed the border into the United States with 480 soldiers and some prisoners to attack the small town of Columbus, New Mexico. Columbus was a settlement struggling to survive in the middle of the desert. It had a hotel, a bank, a drugstore, a clothing store, a church, about 300 inhabitants, and a railroad track that was its only contact with the bigger world. While Columbus was sleeping, three columns of Villistas penetrated the quiet town, shouting, "Viva México!" and "Viva Villa!" According to some witnesses, they also shouted, "Let's kill the gringos!" The villagers began shooting into the houses, forcing entry into commercial establishments, and looting. At the hotel, which was on the second floor of a building, the attackers forced the male guests down the stairs and executed them one by one, while the women watched as the corpses formed a pile in the middle of the street. The attackers seized horses, food, mules, clothing, cigarettes, jewelry, and sweets. The sound of machine guns was heard throughout the town, and the fire was so intense that there was a ghostly glow shifting from one position to another. Archibald Frost and his wife Mary Alice, who had a furniture store, hid in their basement, but they later thought better of it and hurried to their garage to look for their car. When Archibald tried to turn on the engine, the Villistas came and shot him, but he managed to get up and escape. Halfway to Deming, he was bleeding so profusely that his wife Mary Alice had to take the wheel. Behind their backs, they saw the glow of the flames consuming the stores and the Commercial Hotel.

After the initial surprise, the inhabitants of Columbus formed barricades and began to defend themselves. The location of Pancho

Villa during the attack has been the subject of much discussion. Many say that he stayed on the Mexican side, but Maud Wright, a woman who was being held prisoner with the Mexicans and released in Columbus, claimed that Villa was in the middle of the town, screaming, cheering his troops, and striking the fallen or scared soldiers with his saber in order to send them back to the battle. Although the soldiers at the American camp had suspected that Villa was planning something, they reacted painfully late. By dawn, they managed to repel the attackers and chased them beyond the border. Villa, according to witnesses, took off his hat and shook it defiantly, waving goodbye at the American troops who followed him.

In the United States, outrage struck the country like lightning, and strident voices demanded to intervene militarily. Within days, nearly 10,000 soldiers were stationed along the border with Mexico, and the first warplanes began to fly over the state of Chihuahua. Villa's reasons for attacking an insignificant population and killing innocents in the middle of the night have been hotly debated. According to the Villistas themselves, many of them being interviewed decades later when they were old men, Pancho Villa was outraged because he believed that Carranza had sold the country to make it a protectorate of the United States. Villa had promised his men that they would march to Washington. "The United States wants to swallow Mexico: let's see if they'll choke with it in its throat." In any case, Villa could not have been so naive as to think about invading the American Union, but he could take revenge for what he perceived as treason. Others, like the eminent historian Friedrich Katz, see Germany's hand behind the attack, reasoning that the Kaiser was hoping to provoke a war in North America that would divert US resources. A third explanation has been offered, which is that Villa wanted to punish a Columbus arms dealer who sold him defective weapons and contributed to his resounding defeat in Celaya. The final explanation possibly has a combination of the other two mixed in there. The witnesses insist that the Villistas searched everywhere for the arms dealer named Sam Ravel, who, luckily, was in El Paso. There is a mountain of evidence of Villa's involvement with Germany and of his belief that Carranza had sold out to the United States. In 1975, a letter from the time of the attack on Columbus was discovered by Katz. In it, Villa invites Emiliano Zapata to join forces to invade the United States. The most significant extracts say:

My projects were frustrated, because the enemy [Carranza] had the undue and shameless support of the American government...the integrity and independence of our country is about to be lost if we, all honest Mexicans, do not unite in arms to prevent the sale of our homeland, and you must already know about the treaties that Carranza agreed with the Washington Government...Since the movement we have to make against the United States can only be carried out [here] in the north, and in view that we do not have ships, I beg you to tell me if you agree to come here with all your troops, on what date, and I will have the pleasure of personally going to meet you, and together we will undertake the work of rebuilding and ennobling Mexico, and punishing our eternal enemy.

The attack on Columbus represents Villa's lowest point, who was an otherwise heroic figure; it achieved nothing and took innocent lives, and it nearly provoked an international war. In the United States, many outraged and opportunistic voices called for a new intervention to punish Mexico, but with World War I going on in Europe, President Woodrow Wilson knew that the path of prudence was of the utmost importance. However, the US approved an expedition under the command of General John J. Pershing and several thousand men to capture Villa. Carranza also sent a large group of men to hunt down the Centaur of the North.

Illustration 5. The Punitive Expedition.
Photoprint by William Fox, 1916.
Library of Congress, USA.

Pershing's army grew to 10,000 men, who were deployed in three columns that included infantry, cavalry, field artillery, and eight airplanes. The American general led his men 700 miles into Mexico through plains so desolate and monotonous that photos of the expedition remind one of those taken by Roald Amundsen in his journey to the South Pole four years earlier. Pershing's first enemies were frequent dust storms, swarms of flies, and boredom among his troops. "Where is Pancho Villa?" asked Pershing in his broken Spanish in each ranch and village in the mountains, only to get misleading or extremely confusing information from villagers. In several parts of the state of Chihuahua, Pershing found bands of Villistas, and fighting ensued in Ciudad Guerrero at the end of March, in Agua Caliente on April 4th, and Parral on April 11th, with the latter having started by the civilian population attacking the Americans. Pershing's incursion increased Villa's waning popularity among northern Mexicans, who gave Pershing the wrong directions when he asked where the bandit was. These events were followed by an urgent exchange of diplomatic notes and then a conference between Generals Hugo L. Scott, the chief of staff of the United States Army, and Álvaro Obregón.

In a skirmish with a Carrancista general, Francisco Bertani, Villa was wounded in the leg by one of his own men, who tried to betray him when he thought Villa was finished. The Centaur fell from his horse, bleeding, but to his good luck, the enemy did not notice. For almost three months, nothing was heard of him, and the newspapers repeated the rumor that he had died. Carranza sent a party to find Pancho Villa's alleged tomb in the mountains, with the help of guides who claimed to know the location of the makeshift grave. But the Centaur was not dead. His men had taken him with infinite difficulties on the back of a donkey to an ultra-secret cave in the mountains, whose whereabouts were known only by a handful of his most faithful companions. They covered the entrance with branches and left him alone, only visiting to bring food. For six weeks, they fed him with a few handfuls of rice and some sugar, while his broken femur healed. The drinking water had to be collected fifteen kilometers (a little over nine miles) away from the cave. His leg swelled, leaking pus, and the Centaur suffered unspeakably.

Carranza, meanwhile, exerted intense diplomatic pressure to bring Pershing's expedition to an end. In the middle of Chihuahua, numerous Mexican troops gathered with the order to stop the American advance. Pershing was notified but refused to back down. On June 21st, 1916, the armies met. Captain Charles T. Boyd and Mexican General Félix Uresti exchanged warnings and screamed at one another, then withdrew to prepare for battle. The clash was no longer between Pershing's men and Villistas but between the American and Mexican armies. The skirmish lasted more than three hours and strained the binational relations to the breaking point. The hawks in the United States played the drums of war, and President Wilson sent warships to both Mexican coasts.

In the beginning, the peace conferences stalled because Carranza demanded the withdrawal of the American troops as an absolutely necessary condition, while President Wilson, on the other hand, did not want to appear weak before the Mexican government. Finally, a treaty was signed in which the Punitive Expedition would leave the country. The imminent breakdown of relations between the United States and Germany contributed to the settlement. Villa, meanwhile, remained hidden in a cave in the rugged Sierra Madre.

"I have the honor of informing you," Pershing wrote his report at the end of the day, "that Francisco Villa is everywhere and nowhere." The Punitive Expedition returned to the United States without fulfilling its objective. In private, the famous military leader later admitted that "when the true history is written, it will not be a very inspiring chapter for school children, or even grownups to contemplate. Having dashed into Mexico with the intention of eating the Mexicans raw, we turned back at the first repulse and are now sneaking home under cover, like a whipped cur with its tail between its legs." Pershing was probably too hard on himself. Thanks to the Punitive Expedition, the United States stretched its muscles and implemented new tactics, experimented with new weapons in Mexico (including mechanical vehicles instead of cavalry), and, for the first time, deployed its military aircraft. It was a warm-up for what was coming next year. The American generals received good field training, including a young George S. Patton. Pershing would go on to become his country's commander of the American Expeditionary Forces on the Western Front in World War I.

Chapter 13 – The Zimmermann Telegram

In search of legitimacy for his government, Carranza called a Constituent Congress in late 1916 to draft a new constitution. The assembly did not meet in Mexico City but rather in Querétaro, 200 kilometers (almost 125 miles) north of the capital, and it was symbolically chosen for it was the place where the foreign emperor Maximilian of Habsburg was shot. To Carranza's discredit, he did not invite Villistas or Zapatistas, but in an act of poetic justice, many constituents formed a radical and progressive wing—which Carranza had never expected—that incorporated many of Zapata's ideas into the document. It was the legacy of the Convention of Aguascalientes. Many constituents understood that if they did not include progressive reforms, the last seven years of their struggle would have been in vain, and they would be disloyal to thousands and thousands of peasants whose blood had been shed.

The Mexican Constitution was approved on February 5th, 1917, and it was the first in the world to guarantee the social rights of workers and peasants, establishing bases for agrarian reform and empowering the working class. According to the Encyclopedia of World Constitutions, "it can be affirmed that social constitutionalism, or the social democratic rule of law, was modeled by this constitution, and was the inspiration for others, such as the Weimar Constitution of 1919 and the Russian Constitution of 1918." Democracy is not only a political regime but a way of life, founded on constant economic, social, and cultural improvements for the people.

Mexico would have to go a long way to achieve this ideal. The Constitution was only signaling the route they had to take. Meanwhile, the country had the urgent need to end the armed phase of the Mexican Revolution and proceed, as President Plutarco Elías Calles would say a few years later, to a revolution of the minds. In the year of the new Constitution, a puzzling international incident involving Germany, Mexico, and the United States occurred in the final part of the Mexican Revolution, which changed the history of the 20th century. In January of 1917, while the new Constitution was being drafted, the British intelligence service intercepted a telegram sent by German Foreign Secretary Arthur Zimmermann to the German ambassador in Mexico, Heinrich von Eckardt. When the British showed the paper to the US Embassy in London, the Americans thought it was a joke. But once they learned it was authentic, and its content was disseminated in the American press, the American people burned with indignation. In the telegram, Arthur Zimmermann instructed the ambassador to begin negotiations with President Carranza so that, with German support, Mexico could declare war on the US. In return, it would get "generous financial support," and if the Central Powers won World War I, Mexico would recover the states of Texas, New Mexico, and Arizona, the territories it had lost in 1847. The telegram, decoded by the intelligence of Great Britain, said:

We intend to begin on the first of February unrestricted submarine warfare. We shall endeavor in spite of this to keep the United States of America neutral. In the event of this not succeeding, we make Mexico a proposal of alliance on the following basis: make war together, make peace together, generous financial support and an understanding on our part that Mexico is to reconquer the lost territory in Texas, New Mexico, and Arizona. The settlement in detail is left to you. You will inform the President of the above most secretly as soon as the outbreak of war with the United States of America is certain, and add the suggestion that he should, on his own initiative, invite Japan to immediate adherence and at the same time mediate between Japan and ourselves. Please call the President's attention to the fact that the ruthless employment of our submarines now offers the prospect of compelling England in a few months to make peace.

Signed, ZIMMERMANN.

Of course, the telegram was only useful if its contents remained secret to the United States and its allies. After being displayed on the front page of every paper in the world, it became practically useless, a skeleton brought out of the closet. If Carranza learned about its contents from the newspaper like everyone else or through his foreign minister, Cándido Aguilar, it is not known, but it is a fact that the president with the long white beard at least considered the possibility to seize the day and get something from Germany.

Carranza sent his foreign minister, Aguilar, to talk with Heinrich von Eckardt, Berlin's envoy in Mexico City, and ask him whether Germany could provide weapons. A few days after the telegram was disclosed, Germany offered, through Captain Ernst von Hülsen, to provide 30,000 rifles, 100 machine guns, six mountain cannons, and four howitzers. This was clearly not enough to declare war on the United States, but it was enough to create a continental distraction. Von Hülsen knew that it would be impossible to send weapons to Mexico due to the British blockade, so he proposed that instead of ships with hardware, Germany should send cash to Carranza so that he could buy the weapons from South America. An amount of thirty million marks was established, and it is not clear whether this money ever changed hands from Berlin to Mexico City.

Carranza also established a commission to investigate whether Mexico should agree to the more serious terms of the telegram—to join the Central Powers and declare war on the Allies. The Germans promised more money and weapons to help wage war on the United States, but most likely, Carranza was simply playing with the Germans, trying to get funds from whatever source he could in order to consolidate his power with minimal commitment. The Mexican president was not the only man to play with both sides of the equation. Eckardt started meeting secretly with other generals to overthrow Carranza. On April 14th, 1917, Carranza finally declined Zimmermann's proposal, but he did not close all the doors. "If Mexico is dragged into the [First] World War in spite of everything, we'll see. For now the alliance has been frustrated, but it will be necessary later on at a certain moment."

Mexico remained a neutral nation, but the Zimmermann Telegram threw the hitherto neutral US into the First World War, and as a result, the United States turned its attention away from Mexico for good. Carranza was thus firmly established in the presidency. Villa was out of sight, without an army, and being persecuted as a bandit. Obregón had retired into private life in his ranch, and Huerta was dead. There remained only one small nuisance: Zapata, who survived in the south, resisting armed incursions, arsons, and bribes—even the Mexican Air Force found its first military use against the Zapatistas. So, Carranza decided to murder him.

Death of Zapata

Like Villa, Zapata was an international celebrity, a combination of a bandit and a popular hero, a peasant with a huge hat that people looked at with a mix of fear and reverence, a man whom his time did not understand. His recognition as a social fighter would only come after his death. His critics saw him as a threat to order and decency. "Zapata seems to belong to some other century," wrote *The New York Times* in early 1919. "Savage, boastful, fond of loading his person with diamonds and gold, polygamous, a patriarch of banditry, he fulfills the book-and-boy idea of a robber." Zapata had never thought in national terms but rather in local ones. So, while Carranza and his armed hand Obregón took care of Pancho Villa, Zapata was free to materialize his social program and distribute land among the peasants in Morelos.

The state of Morelos, Zapata's headquarters, experienced peace for the first time in years. The peasants, now in possession of their land, no longer planted sugar or rice for the haciendas but corn, beans, chickpeas, onions, and chili peppers for their families. Its communities were reborn in that period, according to John Womack, one of Zapata's most distinguished biographers: "They even refused to allow wood to be cut for railway sleepers and fuel, or give permission to draw water for the locomotives. For the harassed officials of Mexico City this was the work of evil and superstitious peasants. But the Morelians understood the question differently: the old contracts with the haciendas and the railroads were no longer valid; wood and water now belonged to them."

The utopia did not last long. Free from Villa, the Carrancistas went to the south with spies and agitators, and in October 1917, they returned once again with soldiers. Throughout 1918, the Zapatistas, the last rebel faction, suffered a relentless hunt by the army. Anita Brenner commented in her history of the revolution, "In the sugar country Zapata held out against the government's general Pablo Gonzalez, who warred by the 'scorched earth' method—he destroyed every village he thought might harbor Zapatistas, killing all the males." Like Villa, Zapata was a fugitive now. He often used a double for meetings. Some of his men, desperate, took amnesty from the government, while others, disappointed and angry, punished the traitors.

Finally, in April 1919, the army ambushed him. Zapata's men told him rumors that a very apt colonel named Jesús Guajardo had broken with Carranza. Zapata calculated that if he had Guajardo on his side, he could strengthen his thinning army. He sent him a letter with an invitation to join his troops. Guajardo had indeed declared himself to be in rebellion and had taken the town of Jonacatepec, where he shot the traitors to Zapata, but his actions were a carefully planned deception. Zapata was warned by his spies of possible treason, but he ignored them. On April 10th, the southern leader came down from the mountains with an escort of thirty men to meet with Guajardo at the Chinameca hacienda.

The general ordered his men to wait outside; he moved inside with ten guards only. In the courtyard, the soldiers formed a line to present arms. A bugle called three times. When the instrument went silent, all of the men in formation opened fire at the same time. Zapata fell. He was dead, there and then. The news brought great joy to the government but tears to the towns of southern Mexico. Carranza promoted Guajardo to division general and gave him a prize of 50,000 pesos in silver coins.

The body was taken on a mule to Cuautla, the capital of the state of Morelos, where it was photographed and exhibited so that people would be convinced that the southern leader had really died. The prevailing feeling among the common folk was disbelief. Zapata was only 39. One of the few existing photographs of Zapata's corpse when it was on display in the Cuautla main square shows him in his white shirt completely darkened with blood. His expression is peaceful as if he were asleep. His body broken, Zapata lies in the lap of four men—Zapatistas probably—whose expressions are similar to those of saints in a mystical rapture. One of them looks away at the sky, another's chin rests on Zapata's hair, a third reclines his left side on the leader's forehead, and the fourth peasant, with intense indigenous features, looks at the camera with an expression of indignation. Two days later, Zapata was buried in the Cuautla cemetery. According to a reporter who was covering the story, when the funeral procession arrived, there was an unknown elderly woman waiting by the grave, on her knees. The undertakers lowered the coffin, but before they dumped the earth, the woman stood up, took some dust, and threw it on the casket. Then she withdrew, wiping away her tears with the tip of her shawl—a perfect metaphor for the state in which those communities were left.

Zapata's blood-soaked clothes were displayed in a street of Mexico City, outside the premises of a newspaper. Many in Morelos did not buy it; they said that it was, in fact, his double who had been killed, as the body had a scar missing, and the fingers of the corpse were shorter. For many years, even until the 1940s, people in the southern mountains claimed to have seen Zapata on his horse.

Illustration 6. Emiliano Zapata dead.
Unknown photographer, 1919. Originally published
in the newspaper Excelsior, Mexico.

Carranza, now satisfied, had no idea that he would join Zapata in the grave the following year. In 1920, the year of the presidential election, he proposed a civilian as a candidate for the presidency, a virtual unknown surnamed Bonillas. This apparently was the pretext for a group of generals from the north to join a rebellion to remove Carranza. A popular general came to the fore: Álvaro Obregón, who, besides planting more chickpeas, had been meditating on his political ambitions. The rebellion against Carranza, the latest in a long series of ten years, caught like fire on dry grass. In May 1920, the patriarch left the capital with the national treasury bound for Veracruz, as he had once done before, but his time had come. His train derailed, and Carranza dismounted with his most trusted men and continued on horseback, passing some ranches, crossing a river, and finally reaching a place called Tlaxcalantongo. On the night of May 21st, 1920, while sleeping in a hut, a group of traitors on horseback rushed over to his cabin. "Licenciado [lawyer], they broke my leg!" were his last words. The man with the long white beard was dead. In the official story, the traitors killed him, but more recent opinions, based on analysis of his clothes, say that Carranza preferred suicide rather than see himself in the hands of his enemies.

With his death, a cycle was closed. Currently, Carranza was the last president of Mexico to be overthrown or to be unable to finish his term, a fate that practically all of the presidents of Mexico in the last one hundred years before him had gone through. He was also the only president to be killed during his tenure. On December 1st, 1920, exactly ten years after the beginning of the Mexican Revolution—minus ten days—the last player on the field, Álvaro Obregón, assumed the presidency of the republic. Possibly the most skillful general in Mexico's history, Obregón had won all his battles and had finally emerged as the victor in the longest war of his country. And he had only lost one arm.

Chapter 14 – Aftermath

After a decade of fighting and between one and three million deaths (the figure is still disputed), the Mexican Revolution, which had initially started to restore democracy and then to regenerate the country's economy, proved to be the most expensive war and with more casualties in Mexico's history. But the long struggle did raise awareness of the need for social justice, starting with land distribution, labor reform, and education for the people. The ideals promoted by fighters such as Madero, Villa, and especially Zapata were embodied in the new Constitution promulgated in 1917, which still governs the land today.

The Mexican Revolution, a decisive event in the formation of 20th-century Mexico's philosophy, economy, and even artistic development, was, in the words of distinguished historian Alan Knight, one of those "relatively rare episodes in history when the mass of the people profoundly influenced events." It brought the rise of the popular classes and the displacement of the oligarchy that had ruled the country's destiny through almost all of the 19th century. For the first time, the peasants and the working classes were positioned as a real political force with a voice in the country's development. The new state, born in 1920 when the bullets stopped flying and the dust settled, was not democratic in the whole sense of the word, but it was nationalist and popular, not xenophobic; it was revolutionary but with stable institutions. The Mexican Revolution spawned authoritarian leaders, but they were men forged on the battlefield, with a social conscience and willingness to fight for justice and economic equality.

From an economic point of view, the Mexican Revolution was like a second war of independence: it backpedaled the process of big foreign trusts taking over the country's economy. The expression "taking over the country's economy" may seem exaggerated, but looking at Mexico's history through what historians call long-cycle analysis, it is clear that foreign powers, especially the United States, were advancing slowly and inexorably over the country. It was a new form of appropriation, no longer a territorial conquest but economic, through foreign investments and the intensive exploitation of natural resources. In 1910, when Francisco Madero made the call to arms, foreign trusts were controlling Mexican territory and even political decisions, and national workers and companies were increasingly dependent on the US business cycle. Porfirio Díaz tried to slow down that process by approaching Europe, but the Mexican Revolution applied the brakes. The Mexican Revolution influenced other popular movements across the Americas, such as Nicaragua and possibly Cuba.

Diplomatically, the revolution had an achievement as well: always in the shadow of the most powerful country in the world, the United States, the Mexican Revolution freed Mexico from America's hand. In the words of Frank Tannenbaum, one of the first historians of the Mexican Revolution in the 1930s, it brought home "the recognition that Mexicans were masters in their own house," putting an end to the fear, which had always been present, of being absorbed by the first world power on the planet.

Most of the great original revolutionaries did not live to see the result of their struggle, but its younger followers, those who rode with Madero, Villa, and Zapata—people like Lázaro Cárdenas, Salvador Alvarado, and José Vasconcelos—created the new Mexican nation.

After a hundred years of calamities, the country found a route that could accommodate everyone.

Epilogue – The Head of Pancho Villa and the Hand of Obregón

And what happened to Pancho Villa? In 1920, when his enemy Carranza died, Villa was a shadow of the great general who once had swept Mexico. For four years, he traveled the roads and passages between the mountains of northern Mexico with a few hundred men, robbing and breaking into estates and villages to survive. The Americans wanted him and put a price on his head; the Carrancistas wanted him too, and the new leaders of Mexico—Álvaro Obregón and his men from Sonora—distrusted him. Villa could be an outlaw, but he was the last great heavyweight of the revolution still alive, and he had demonstrated his ability to summon people around him. The provisional president, Adolfo de la Huerta, raised the reward for Pancho Villa, dead or alive.

In 1920, Villa decided to negotiate. A meeting was arranged, but when the government envoy tried to kill him, Villa proclaimed that things had not changed and that he was going to continue the fight. However, he was certain that the new generation did not know what to do with him, whether to kill him or render honors to him. He crossed the desert, seized more weapons and provisions where nobody expected to see him, and, from a position of strength, he made a new proposal to President Adolfo de la Huerta. The president, eager to pacify the north, offered him the hacienda of Canutillo and a personal escort of fifty men paid by the government, although he demanded that Pancho withdraw completely from political activities. Although reluctant at first, Álvaro Obregón, who in a few months would be the new president of Mexico, accepted the pact and made peace with Villa. The US government welcomed the deal because that meant that peace would finally come to Mexico. To the relief of the Mexican government, the United States did not request the extradition of Pancho Villa. The only one to protest bitterly was Britain's secretary of war, Winston Churchill, who called him a murderer and launched threats against Mexico if justice was not sought for the death of a British citizen in 1914.

Villa marched triumphantly with his last men from Coahuila to Durango to enter his safe haven, where he would spend his last years as a simple farmer. Many people went out to see him and cheer him on his march. That man had swept all of northern Mexico in response to Madero's call; he had barely escaped from being shot by Victoriano Huerta, had fled from a prison in Mexico City, had formed the largest army in the history of his country. He had sat in the presidential chair and had despised it, had become America's dearest only to later fall from its grace, and had invaded the United States and became a desperado persecuted by the US Army. But deep in his heart, he had the dream that once the dictators fell and justice was done for the people, he could withdraw and "grow corn and raise cattle until I die among my companions who have suffered so much with me" according to his words to journalist John Reed. "They used to call me a bandit, and I suppose some still call me that," he said to another journalist, Edmond Behr. "My heart is clean. My sole ambition was to disburden Mexico from the [social] class that has oppressed it, and to give the people a chance to know what real liberty means."

The last 800 Villistas surrendered their weapons to the federal government, and Villa occupied a 64,000-hectare hacienda in the state of Durango, a well-watered and fertile area, far away enough to provide him with some protection. Throughout his entire career, he had made enough enemies to know that his safety was one of the most delicate elements to consider. At the hacienda, Villa and his men rebuilt the decayed buildings, stables, and cellars. They put in telephone lines, a mill, and a school for 300 students for the dozens of children Villa had with different wives, plus his soldiers' children and those of the neighboring towns. He baptized the school with the name of Felipe Ángeles, his late faithful general. "If I were in charge of things," he told journalist Frazier Hunt, "I would build a lot of schools in cities and towns, and I would also put a school in every ranch." Sometimes Villa would be present in the classroom and asked teachers to read biographies of famous men to him. Another journalist who visited the hacienda saw that Dante's Divine *Comedy* and a geography text were among his bedside books.

Villa imposed strict conditions on everyone who lived in the Canutillo hacienda. The bell rang at four o'clock in the morning, and everybody had to work the land. Villa supervised the work and sometimes took the yoke himself. He severely punished any robbery with execution. He told his men that he wanted to be able to leave a bag of gold in one place and find it in the same place when he returned, and he warned them that if he had taught them to kill and steal, he wanted them to rehabilitate. *The New York Times* recorded, "Pancho Villa, the former bandit, is a peace-loving, hard-working contented rancher, without political ambitions and imbued with a sincere desire to help his people." True to his word, he stayed away from politics, and if any conspirators visited him to talk him into starting another revolution, he turned them over to Álvaro Obregón. The one-armed man of Celaya was pleased with these signs of obedience from the only general who could cast a shadow on him. Unlike his boss Carranza, Obregón was a practical man with a political nose, a sense of opportunity, and an unchallenged personal charisma. When he came to the presidency in 1920—with a more prominent belly, receding hairline, and a pointed mustache that was beginning to turn white—he was no longer the handsome general of the Mexican Revolution who had won his battles with his army of indomitable Yaqui. But he kept his ability to navigate difficult waters.

In 1922, when more generals were preparing for the presidential elections, Villa, a living legend, made the mistake of talking about politics with a journalist. Even worse, he launched a veiled threat. "I am a real soldier," he said. "I can mobilize 40,000 soldiers in 40 minutes. There are thousands of Mexicans who are still my followers." And then he gave his support to candidate Adolfo de la Huerta, the man who had pardoned him, and not to Plutarco Elías Calles, the president's appointed candidate. On July 20th, 1923, Villa got into his car with a reduced escort of four and headed for the city of Parral, eighty kilometers (almost fifty miles) away. Villa and his guards noticed that the streets of Parral were unusually deserted. At some point, an old man passed in front of the car, shouting, "Viva Villa!" and then shots were heard from all directions, piercing the vehicle. Villa was shot four times, but just to be sure, one of his assassins went to the shattered Ford and put a bullet into his head. A horrified girl of thirteen saw the scene, and she ran through the streets of Parral, crying, "They just shot Pancho Villa!" The man who was believed to have been invincible lay with his body pierced in a horrific position, half of it coming out of the car's window. The corpse was exhibited at the Hotel Hidalgo in Parral. Someone had taken off his shirt, and the expression on his face is of deep exhaustion.

Villa was buried in Parral, but even after his death, he demonstrated that he could be, as Pershing would say, everywhere and nowhere. In 1926, they found the grave had been violated, the coffin destroyed. The body was there, but the head had been removed. It was never recovered. Who was interested in the head of Pancho Villa? Theories range from the American government, Yale University, an auction house, and one of Villa's multiple enemies. Villa's reputation remained as a bandit in official history until the 1970s, after enough time had passed, when the rest of the body was exhumed and taken to a place of honor in Mexico City: the emblematic Monument to the Revolution. Or so they thought. In 1931, one of his widows, fearing that grave robbers would continue to desecrate his tomb and body, placed Villa's remains in an unmarked grave and replaced them with an anonymous woman who had died of cancer at the Parral hospital. When they opened the tomb in 1976, they found jewelry and fragments of a woman's dress.

The hand that Álvaro Obregón had lost in his final confrontation with Villa in central Mexico also had a macabre adventure. When his doctor Enrique Osornio amputated the arm on the battlefield, among the flying bullets, he kept the general's hand in a jar with formalin. The hand reached the state of Sinaloa, and not knowing what to do with it, the doctor gave it to a military friend of Obregón's, who told him that he was not very interested in hanging onto it. In a strange twist of fate, the jar was stolen by a prostitute, and the severed hand ended up in a brothel in downtown Mexico City, where it was found years later by the same doctor who amputated the arm. He took it and gave it to a former collaborator of Obregón, who convinced President Lázaro Cárdenas (1934–1940) to build a monument for the hand in the restaurant where Obregón was assassinated in 1928. The restaurant was demolished, and the place became a macabre mausoleum that displayed the leader's right hand, which, by then, was already yellow, crimped, misshapen, and inflated like a balloon. It stayed there for many years until his descendants, surely horrified by that unspeakable monument, requested the hand and cremated it in 1989.

The "villain" of this story, Victoriano Huerta, rests in a modest grave in the Evergreen Cemetery in El Paso, Texas, less than one mile away from the border, still unable to reach his country. At night, the tomb is visited by members of El Paso paranormal associations because they attribute powers to it and believe that, from the grave, Huerta continues to emanate "evil forces."

In some way, the strange story of Pancho Villa's head, Obregón's hand, and Huerta's grave are all metaphors for the Mexican

Revolution: its heroes and villains, dead and buried, their exploits and felonies, now extinguished, continue to inspire respect, fear, curiosity, and devotion. Just like the Mexican Revolution. The revolutionaries' bones might be in a monument, or they might be lost, perhaps appropriated by the state, institutionalized, or forgotten under a humble tombstone, but the men's ideals and lessons, one hundred years after the end of the storm, remain intact.

Bibliography

Blaisdell, L. "Henry Lane Wilson and the Overthrow of Madero." *The Southwestern Social Science Quarterly*, 1962.

Brenner, Anita. *The Wind that Swept Mexico*. University of Texas Press, 1971.

Gilly, Adolfo. *The Mexican Revolution*. The New Press, 2005.

Katz, Friedrich. *The Life and Times of Pancho Villa*. Stanford University Press, 1998.

Katz, Friedrich. *The Secret War in Mexico*. University of Chicago, 1984.

Knight, Alan. *The Mexican Revolution*, Vol 1-3. University of Nebraska Press, 1990.

Meyer, M. "The Mexican-German Conspiracy of 1915." *The Americas*, 23(1), 76-89, 1966.

Meyer, M. *Huerta*. University of Nebraska Press, 1972.

Mraz, John. *Photographing the Mexican Revolution. Commitments, Testimonies, Icons*. University of Texas Press, 2012.

Reed, John. *Insurgent Mexico*. Red and Black Publishers, 2009.

Welsome, Eileen. *The General and the Jaguar: Pershing's Hunt for Pancho Villa: A True Story of Revolution and Revenge*. Little, Brown and Company, 2009.

Womack, John. *Zapata and the Mexican Revolution*. Vintage, 2011.

Guzmán, Martín Luis. *The Eagle and the Serpent.*

Knight, Alan. (1990) *The Mexican Revolution.* Vol 1-3. University of Nebraska Press.

Tuchman, Barbara. (1985) *The Zimmermann Telegram.* Random House.

Escalante, Pablo *et al. Nueva Historia Mínima de México.* Mexico: El Colegio de México, 2004.

Gussinyer i Alfonso, Jordi. *México-Tenochtitlan en una Isla. Introducción al urbanismo de una ciudad precolombina.* Spain: Universitat de Barcelona, 2001.

Katz, Friedrich. *The Secret War in Mexico: Europe, the United States, and the Mexican Revolution.* Chicago: University of Chicago Press, 1984.

Khasnabish, Alex. *Zapatistas: Rebellion from the Grassroots to the Global.* Canada: Fernwood Publishing Ltd, 2010.

León-Portilla, Miguel. *El México Antiguo en la Historia Universal.* Mexico: FOEM, 2015.

León-Portilla, Miguel. *The Broken Spears: The Aztec Account of the Conquest of Mexico.* Boston: Beacon Press, 2006.

Meyer, Jean. *La Cristiada. The Mexican People´s War for Religious Liberty.* New York: SquareOne Publishers, 2013.

Restall, Matthew. *When Montezuma Met Cortes: The True Story of the Meeting that Changed History.* New York: HarperCollins, 2018.

Schulenburg, Mariana. *Guadalupe: Visión y Controversia.* Aguascalientes: Libros de México: 2016.

Vázquez Lozano, Gustavo. *The Aztec Eagles. The History of the Mexican Pilots Who Fought in World War II.* Aguascalientes: Libros de Mexico, 2019.

Here's another book by Captivating History that you might be interested in

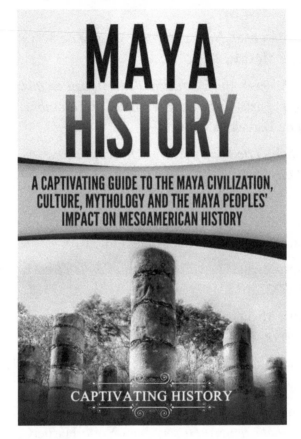

CPSIA information can be obtained
at www.ICGtesting.com
Printed in the USA
LVHW101313010922
727306LV00004B/432

9 781647 488048